THE SOUL'S JOURNEY

An Artist's Approach to the
Stations of the Cross
Artwork and Text by Kathrin Burleson

THE SOUL'S JOURNEY

An Artist's Approach to the
Stations of the Cross
Artwork and Text by Kathrin Burleson

Forward Movement, Cincinnati, Ohio

© Artwork by Kathrin Burleson
Book design by Higherworks, Cincinnati, Ohio

© 2014 by Forward Movement

Library of Congress Cataloging-in-Publication Data

Burleson, Kathrin, 1950- author, illustrator.
The soul's journey : an artist's approach to the Stations of the Cross
/ Kathrin Burleson.
pages cm
"Artwork and Text by Kathrin Burleson. With reflections by
the Most Rev. Katharine Jefferts Schori, the Rt. Rev. Barry Beisner,
Sister Teresa Martin, CT, the Rev. Albert R. Cutie, the Rev. Scott Gunn, and
Friar Leo Joseph, OSF."

ISBN 978-0-88028-390-8 (alk. paper)
1. Stations of the Cross. I. Title.
BX2040.B87 2014
232.96--dc23

2014020816

Printed in USA

www.forwardmovement.org

DEDICATION

This book is dedicated to Friar Leo M. Joseph, OSF

CONTENTS

ix FOREWORD

xi INTRODUCTION

2 STATION I – ACCEPTANCE
Jesus Prays in the Garden of Gethsemane
Bishop Barry Beisner

8 STATION II – BETRAYAL
Jesus is Betrayed and Arrested
Presiding Bishop Katharine Jefferts Schori

14 STATION III – DENIAL
Peter Denies Jesus
Father Alberto R. Cutié

20 STATION IV – JUDGMENT
The Crowd Condemns Jesus
Bishop Barry Beisner

26 STATION V – HUMILIATION
The Soldiers Mock Jesus
Sister Teresa Marie Martin, CT

32 STATION VI – SUFFERING
Jesus Carries His Cross
Father Scott Gunn

38 STATION VII – HELP
Simon of Cyrene Assists Jesus
Father Scott Gunn

44 STATION VIII – WITNESS
Jesus Meets the Women of Jerusalem
Friar Leo M. Joseph, OSF

50 STATION IX – SURRENDER
Soldiers Nail Jesus to the Cross
Friar Leo M. Joseph, OSF

56 STATION X – COMPASSION
Mary and the Beloved Disciple Stand at the Foot of the Cross
Father Alberto R. Cutié

62 STATION XI – DEATH
Jesus Dies on the Cross
Friar Leo M. Joseph, OSF

68 STATION XII – LOVE
Jesus' Body is Taken Down from the Cross
Friar Leo M. Joseph, OSF

74 STATION XIII – WAITING
Jesus' Body is Entombed
Presiding Bishop Katharine Jefferts Schori

80 STATION XIV – RESURRECTION
The Lord is Risen
Sister Teresa Marie Martin, CT

87 ABOUT THE ARTIST
89 ABOUT THE CONTRIBUTORS
93 ACKNOWLEDGEMENTS

FOREWORD

When I agreed to paint the Stations of the Cross, I knew I would be taking on a large commitment of time and work. What I didn't realize was how far reaching the effects would be and how personal the project would become. Over the course of about a year, as I studied scripture, drew, wrote, and painted, I experienced the stations in a very different way. In the past I had been in the role of observer; this time I needed to relate to each station as a participant. Before I could hope to capture the essence of the story, I needed to experience the point of view of each person and try to imagine his or her feelings. Isn't that how stories touch us? When we relate to the characters, we enter the drama. The Stations of the Cross give us the opportunity to enter the drama, to be a part of this journey from life to death to life, to let ourselves be transformed by the story and to make it our own. *The Soul's Journey* invites you to walk the Stations of the Cross in new ways. Consider the passages from scripture, reflect upon the meditations offered by leading theologians, bishops, and priests, and explore the winding path of an artist as I share the deep soul searching and inspiration that led to the creation of each of these fourteen stations. Psalm 19 captures my hope for you: "Let the words of my mouth and the meditation of my heart be acceptable in your sight, O Lord, my strength and my redeemer."

May it be so.

KATHRIN BURLESON
SUMMER, 2014

INTRODUCTION

The project of painting a series of the Stations of the Cross started despite me. As an Episcopalian, I had a friendly but distant relationship with the Stations of the Cross. When this liturgy was offered at church once a year, generally on Good Friday, I would dutifully show up with a handful of others and spend an hour or so walking the stations.

I learned that the tradition of walking the Way of the Cross, or the Stations of the Cross as it has come to be known, dates back to the earliest centuries of Christianity. Many Christians desired to make a pilgrimage to Jerusalem to follow in the steps of Jesus on his last days. But for most, this was an impossible dream. Consequently, churches and communities established the tradition of walking the stations as a devotional ritual in their locale.

At my church, there was no permanent installation of the stations, so we would use small black and white reproductions taped on the wall of the nave. On these occasions, I felt as if I were merely going through the motions of a ritual. Hearing the scripture, reading the response, spending a few minutes in reflection—the experience always stayed right at the surface for me. I never felt as if I were involved in the drama. In retrospect, this was in large part because I never knew which role I was playing, which perspective was mine. Was I an observer? A perpetrator? Was I to be experiencing the agony of Jesus? Was I to be a mourner, a disciple, a Pharisee? Or all of the above? Not knowing my place, I stayed firmly rooted in myself, unable to relate to any of it. My mind wandered, and I paid more attention to my fellow travelers than I did to the narrative of Jesus' path from arrest to death to resurrection. I was distracted and unfocused. For many years, my relationship with the Stations of the Cross was as a distant observer.

One exception was many years ago when I experienced the stations at the beginning of a Cursillo weekend. Cursillo, a spiritual renewal weekend, took place at the fairgrounds at Ferndale, a nearby dairy town. It was nighttime, and the stations had been set up at various spots on the fairgrounds. After each scripture and reading, participants took turns dragging a large wooden cross from station to station. The experience was very earthy and real. In the misty darkness, I could hear the wood scrape as the cross was dragged across the rough ground. One of the participants was handicapped and wore a leg brace, and you could hear the metal of the brace drag as she struggled with each step. At the crucifixion station, a spike was hammered into the cross. Bam! Bam! Bam!

This time, the readings were no longer about a historical incident; they were about us, this ragtag group of pilgrims gathered to take a deeper look at our Christian walk. I was forced out of my role as observer and into the role of participant. The hands-on experience and sensory input made the stations come alive. Through changing our perspective and involving our senses and bodies, we entered the world of metaphor. This was our journey, and the trials, betrayals, and helpers we encounter along the way.

The following Holy Week, there I was at church, walking through the stations with the usual small group, trying to find some meaning and response to the exercise. Nothing. Eventually, I decided the Stations of the Cross simply weren't a meaningful part of my devotions so I quit going. From then on, my encounters with the stations were limited to visits to Roman Catholic churches, and even then I would usually look at them from a formal perspective, as decoration or art.

Imagine my surprise when the priest of my parish informed me that a benefactor had requested I paint the Stations of the Cross for the church. I don't do stations, I said. How about an icon? The benefactors want an icon as well, he replied. But they also want the Stations of the Cross, and they want you to paint them.

I am an artist but not a literal painter. I create icons, but they are generally not traditional icons. I incorporate elements of personal imagery into my paintings, so they are difficult to categorize. I have been known to paint icons of animals, which, in certain Christian circles, puts me in a rather dubious position as an iconographer. There is a certain humor and levity in much of my work, so I really didn't think I was the best choice. But I also don't turn away from a challenge. So I accepted the commission.

Months passed as I pondered the project. I read scripture and acquired lots of books about the Stations of the Cross. Some were straightforward explanations of the history and meaning of the stations. Other sources applied the stations to contemporary social justice issues. The reading was interesting, but no approach really resonated with me. Plus, I simply didn't see how I could add anything to what had already been painted or written. I mean, how many ways could these images be presented? It seemed that it had already been done.

I was also concerned about format and materials. Should they be large? Or would that seem overwhelming and dominate the church space? On the other hand, small reproductions are usually too small to see from more than three feet away. These mullings stretched over weeks and then months. I tried a few approaches, but they felt contrived or tired. The iconic depictions seemed too stiff. The painterly narratives were too literal. I was going down a lot of dead-end roads.

Then one day I realized the obvious. I didn't have to paint figures in a historical or even contemporary context. I didn't have to paint figures at all. The ongoing relevance of the Stations of the Cross is in part because the story continues, unfolds, in each of our lives, over and over again. It is a metaphor for the human journey. Metaphor. How could that have eluded me for so long?

These stations could never replicate my Cursillo experience. After all, those were real people carrying a real cross, creating sensory inputs that just couldn't happen in the nave of a church. And yet even that experience was not about some remote historical event. It was about our own journeys. That experience of the Stations of the Cross spoke to me because I participated in the drama, incorporated the symbols, and found my own places of betrayal, pain, and redemption. In other words, I entered the metaphor.

This realization changed my whole approach to the project. In my journal/sketchbook, I wrote out the scriptures for each station and then spent time imagining the scene. In particular, I looked for images and phrases I had overlooked before and played around with them in words and in images.

I started each morning with a few words and sketches, and they served as my preparation for the day ahead. They quickly came to replace my other morning devotions and meditation. I had meant this to be the starting point, material that I would draw from when I did the "real" stations. Instead I had the realization that these in fact were my stations. They came from a place of feeling, of abstraction and of metaphor that is where I find my spiritual reality. Ironically, they started with doodles.

As I moved through this process, I was transformed. Rather than being an observer or character in the drama of the Passion, I realized that every life holds aspects of the Passion of Christ.

No longer were the stations part of a story that happened centuries ago, but the events became metaphors for what has happened and what is happening in my own life and the lives of all of us. Abandonment, betrayal, denial…we've all experienced these emotions. I have abandoned those that I love, been abandoned by those I trusted, and abandoned the truth that I know to be myself. I have turned my back on God. In that respect, Peter and I have a lot in common.

The traditional Stations of the Cross were established around the seventeenth century. These fourteen scenes or stations include some drawn from long-standing custom but not directly described in scripture. For instance, the sixth station recounts Jesus' encounter with a woman who wipes his face. The legend of this meeting with the woman, Veronica, describes how she wipes his face with her veil and later discovers that a perfect image of Christ's face remains on the cloth. The name Veronica actually means true image. Since I am an iconographer, I was tempted to include this station, as the legend explains the creation of an early icon. Instead I chose to select as stations those encounters that are explicitly described in scripture. I am not the first artist to do so. Other writers and artists have reimagined the Stations of the Cross in numerous ways. I also included some scenes that are not often a part of the traditional Stations of the Cross, most notably, the first and second in this series—Jesus praying in the Garden of Gethsemane and his betrayal by Judas. Traditional stations generally start with Jesus appearing before Pilate, so this look at Christ's Passion spends more time and puts more emphasis on Jesus' relationships—both with God and with his disciples. I find these stations to be critical as they set the stage for the drama that is about to unfold and emphasize that his relationships with God and his friends are central, sustaining components to the narrative.

These paintings and meditations don't replace traditional depictions of the stations but rather offer another perspective. Narrative images are important to our understanding of the events of Holy Week, but they are not the only lens through which to view the story. This series draws imagery from scripture as well as personal experience. The varying perspectives for each station give the viewer an opportunity to relate to multiple roles—those of observer, betrayed and betrayer, judge and judged, and so on. Each of us has a role in every aspect of this drama, and entering these roles presents other ways to enter into the reality of the living Christ. My hope is that in reading these meditations and reflecting upon the images, that you will relate the Passion of Christ to your own walk, to the soul's journey that shapes each of our lives.

KATHRIN BURLESON

THE SOUL'S JOURNEY

An Artist's Approach to the
Stations of the Cross
Artwork and Text by Kathrin Burleson

I

JESUS PRAYS IN THE GARDEN OF GETHSEMANE

He came out and went, as was his custom, to the Mount of Olives; and the disciples followed him. When he reached the place, he said to them, "Pray that you may not come into the time of trial." Then he withdrew from them about a stone's throw, knelt down, and prayed, "Father, if you are willing, remove this cup from me; yet, not my will but yours be done." When he got up from prayer, he came to the disciples and found them sleeping because of grief; and he said to them, "Why are you sleeping? Get up and pray that you may not come into the time of trial."

– Luke 22:39-46

Scripture tells us often of Jesus in prayer: going off by himself to pray, praying in crowds, praying in moments of ministry, teaching his disciples to pray. He is very much a man of prayer. It is as natural and important to him as breathing. It is what he does because it goes to the heart of who he is, and why he exists; it is why the divine light shines so brightly in him.

Jesus goes to the garden that night to pray. He has spent his whole life getting ready for what is about to happen. He has boldly gone about the work God has given him to do, and he has made powerful enemies in the process. Now they are closing in on him. Very soon he will be in their hands and at their mercy. He knows they will be furiously cruel. He knows that once it gets started, there will be no way out. Everything meaningful about his life—life itself—is on the line this night.

We are shown a light in the darkness of the garden. Here, Jesus struggles for light amidst the deep darkness of desolation, a time of profound loneliness, fear, and uncertainty. It is very hard for us to see this.

We want a Messiah who has no doubts—not someone like us. But Jesus is like us. Tempted in every way as we are, and every bit as vulnerable. Jesus is not a superhuman above all fears and frailties; he must struggle—agonize—to master these emotions, just like

any of us. He must work through these fears and uncertainties to a place of trust in God and obedience to the will of God. Jesus must trust God completely, every step of the way, come what may—just like us. And, just as we must, he does this through prayer.

Scripture shows us a savior who knows us better than we know ourselves, who loves us and forgives us, and who not only teaches us how to pray but also prays himself: *Father. Not my will but yours. Save us from the time of trial.*

In Jesus, we see a light that shines even in that garden, in the darkness of that night, and everywhere. In our own times of crisis, Jesus is with us. Teaching us how to pray. Teaching us to love, trust, and obey God in all things. Not in certitude, but in faith, in a relationship of love and trust. Leading us in the way we need to go. Drinking the cup with us. Inviting us to watch and pray with him.

BISHOP BARRY BEISNER

ACCEPTANCE

I can relate to the disciples who were sleeping, unwilling or unable to be with their Lord. Unfortunately, this is familiar territory for me. But looking at and understanding Jesus' aloneness is harder, perhaps because it is deeper and hurts more.

The pain he is about to endure is beyond my experience or understanding. It is too much. Ultimately we see that Jesus doesn't look for support from friends, from people for whom it might be "too much." He finds his strength from within, through his faith in God.

As an artist, I selected the perspective of Jesus for this station to emphasize his humanity. I wanted to explore the sense of isolation and fear that he must have experienced. Walking closely with God can be scary business, and as Jesus discovers, your whole world can get turned upside down. Home may not be as comfortable and inviting as it once was. Walking with God can cost you friends, family, even your life.

Jesus goes to the Mount of Olives to pray—"as was his custom." For Jesus, prayer is not just offered at times of fear or of danger; it is a constant and integral part of his life. He tells the disciples to pray so they may avoid difficulties and trials. Jesus is asking them for faithfulness. He repeats the command when he returns to wake them up: "Get up and pray." Jesus offers a model for faithfulness. He doesn't go to the garden to get away or to hide. He goes to face his destiny, to pray and to know God's will. As Jesus prays, he seeks the assurance of God's presence and confirms his acceptance of God's will. After Jesus acknowledges his acceptance of God's will—"Not my will but yours be done," the angel of the Lord appears to Jesus, giving him strength (Luke 22:42-43).

A eucharistic prayer comes to mind: "Deliver us from the presumption of coming to this Table for solace only, and not for strength."

Several years ago, my spiritual support group discussed this prayer. We called ourselves the *Gyrovagues*, after the monks that Saint Benedict described as drifters who, among other things, never settle down and are slaves to their own wills. We fit that description quite well. In fact, I still do. In prayer, I often catch myself asking for my will to be done, rather than God's: I seek the easy way out, a painless solution to my problems. It doesn't always occur to me to seek comfort or strength in Jesus during the Eucharist. I too often passively accept whatever the experience offers. The words and actions of Jesus in this scene remind me that I, once again, miss the point. Jesus asks God for what he wants, but then Jesus is clear that he accepts God's will, however painful that may be. He commands his followers to do the same. That instruction applies to us, just as it did to his followers.

The angel who appears to Jesus is not mentioned in the other gospel accounts of the visit to the garden. So when I read the passage in Luke, the angel's presence in the garden jumps off the page. Of course! For me, this apparition, this appearance of the angel, is central to the story. Your friends may let you down, you may feel totally alone and frightened, danger could loom ahead, yet there, just behind the trees in the glimmer of light, is a messenger of hope, the assurance of the Divine Presence. The angel doesn't promise miracles or an easy way out—the angel gives Jesus strength and comfort.

How often have we overlooked the angels in our lives? How many messengers of God have we ignored or simply not seen because we were focused on the wrong things? I had to read and reread scripture before I discovered the importance of the angel as comforter and companion. It sometimes takes a while for me to recognize the presence of angels in my daily life as well. Although I suspect most people are not aware that they are angels for me, when they offer kindness, compassion, and encouragement, they become tangible manifestations of God's grace in the world.

When the angel appears to Jesus, he prays more earnestly. He finds his strength in prayer. The image of his sweat falling to the ground like great drops of blood takes us directly to the crown of thorns and the agony of the Crucifixion. Jesus accepts his destiny, and his prayer is deep and heartfelt. He is fully open to God. Deep prayer, full communication with God, takes each of us beyond the moment and encompasses all that we have been and will be. It removes the interference of the ego, the hanging on to the minutia of the moment, and allows us to experience the fullness of the divine.

When I first truly encountered and accepted the Christian faith over thirty years ago, my beliefs were much different than they are now. I had been a nominal Christian all of my life, but the moment of commitment came when I was in my early twenties. It was a time of change and uncertainty, as I was just out of college and still figuring out what I should do with my life. I was considering marriage and a move halfway across the United States. It was a time of big decisions, and I did not have many tools or much support to guide me. A friend encouraged me to come to church—and she kept after me until I finally agreed to join her one Sunday. While the particular church wasn't where I ended up attending regularly, the visit helped connect to my faith. With the support from those dear, caring, people, I learned that Christ really can and does manifest in community.

Those early years in the church were full of surprises and easy assurances that God was active in my life. Faith nearly became certainty, and predictably, this proved to be a faulty assumption. As years passed and life unfolded, things didn't always turn out the way I anticipated. Eventually, I learned to accept that God's help doesn't always come in ways we expect. In fact, from our limited perspective, sometimes God's help doesn't seem to come at all. But over the years, life experience and study have shown me that God is present in everything, even if sometimes only as a faint glimmer of hope behind a tree.

Many years ago, I became an associate of the Community of the Transfiguration, a women's religious community within The Episcopal Church. In addition to commitments of prayer and support for the Community, each associate is asked to write a personal rule of life, a guide for word, action, and prayer. As I worked on my rule, I had a hard time getting beyond the very basic rule of seeing God in everything. Beyond that, I thought what is there? There is more, held Sister Alice, my mentor and spiritual director. To prod me along, she shared Ninian's Catechism with me. Saint Ninian was an early Anglican bishop in Gallway and along with Patrick, one of the links of continuity between the ancient Roman-British church and early Celtic Christianity.

Today, a copy of the catechism is tacked on the wall above my desk, a reminder that life is more than just understanding one's immediate experience and intuition. Study and discipline inform and help to shape our world. This little catechism inspires me to study more faithfully, and consequently, to recognize the links between scripture, tradition, and the seemingly mundane moments of life. The angels are always there, but when I remember the angel who appeared to Jesus in the garden, I am also reminded me to look more closely at the trees around me and to take the time, with faith, to see the messengers who are with me, even when I don't know it.

Ninian's Catechism

Q: What is best in this world?
A: To do the will of our Maker.

Q: What is his will?
A: That we should live according to the laws of his creation.

Q: How do we know those laws?
A: By study—study the scriptures with devotion.

Q: What tool has our Maker provided for this study?
A: The intellect which can probe everything.

Q: And what is the fruit of study?
A: To perceive the eternal Word of God reflected in every plant and insect, every bird and animal, and every man and woman.

When Jesus rises to leave, knowing that his betrayal is at hand, he asks his friends to be with him, to pray, and to be faithful. This is all he asks of us as well—pray, have faith, and don't turn away from God.

PRAYER

" Divine Protector, send your holy angels to watch over me. Strengthen me in times of darkness, and open my eyes that I may always be aware of your loving presence. **Amen.** "

JESUS IS BETRAYED II
AND ARRESTED

Immediately, while he was still speaking, Judas, one of the twelve, arrived; and with him there was a crowd with swords and clubs, from the chief priests, the scribes, and the elders. Now the betrayer had given them a sign, saying, "The one I will kiss is the man; arrest him and lead him away under guard." So when he came, he went up to him at once and said, "Rabbi!" and kissed him. Then they laid hands on him and arrested him.

– Mark 14:43-46

Betrayal is above all an act of passion. It can never be an apathetic response, a deed of carelessness or ignorance, in the same way that hate is not the opposite of love, neither is betrayal. Judas makes his commitment out of passion, though we're never quite sure what has hold of his heart.

The heart of God is grievously wounded, and this image does justice to the explosion and exploitation unleashed in Judas's passion. And yet, at the same time, the beating heart of the Divine continues to give life to the world—for the passion that underlies all creation will not cease, in spite of bent intention and bodies broken.

The dendritic fingers reaching into the heart's core, or growing out of it, are sign and sacrament of the ceaseless action of the holy. Are they divine yearning for greater and more abundant life? Lament at life misused and diverted? The already-growing greenness of healing and resurrection? Are these tendrils like the placental exchange embracing and enlivening new creation in the womb, in spite of the apparent cost to the one who harbors new life?

The kiss of Judas cannot remain wholly corrupted in the heart of God's intention. It will pass into death, and through it, but it will not end there. The crowd's swords and clubs may seek death and destruction, not knowing that this death will never yield the finality they seek. The hands laid violently on the Rabbi may seek to subvert his passion, but they cannot extinguish it, for its source is in the heart of God. Hands are meant to heal, not harm, to bless and not to bloody, to bring forth life from the womb, and the passion behind the seekers of destruction will not disappear into nothingness. Its chaotic energy will ultimately be turned and redeemed for creative life in the depths of the divine heart.

How will we receive hands, or kisses, or words that seek less than the life-giving gift of the Holy One? Can we see the possibility for divine passion buried within warped attempts to subvert life? And in the depths of our own vulnerability, can our will yield misdirected passion to the greater and only source of life? Will we participate in the transformation of passion?

PRESIDING BISHOP
KATHARINE JEFFERTS SCHORI

BETRAYAL

During the lengthy process of contemplating each station, this was perhaps the most challenging. How could I create the image of someone who has one of the most heinous roles imaginable? One of Jesus' closest and dearest friends has turned him over to his enemies and ultimately to death.

When I began my reflection on this station, I focused on Judas as a greedy and ungrateful man who betrayed his friend. But soon I realized this focus didn't move me beyond judgment and outrage. Yes, Judas was a traitor. But what else? And where did I fit into the story?

I began to realize how tempting it is for us to focus on faults of other people, to wonder about their motivations or to get caught up in their stories. When I have been let down or betrayed, I usually let emotions of sorrow and anger govern my response instead of considering the larger picture. It is entirely too easy to spend my energy judging the perceived perpetrator. Yet, all this does is hook me into a situation that I can do nothing about; this

judgment keeps me firmly in a place with no exit, a place where it is all about me. When we get caught in the need to blame or condemn, we get stuck.

As I opened my heart to the subject of betrayal, I thought about people who had betrayed me over the years. Much to my dismay, I remembered them all too well. As many of the painful details came flooding back, I found myself slipping into the same sense of indignation and hurt that I had experienced many years ago. What a disappointment to realize I had hung on to and nurtured those hurts and those feelings for all of those years. Forgiveness? I thought I had forgiven, but if that were the case, how could the hurts be so easily resurrected? Isn't this a betrayal on my part? A betrayal of my faith and of the example of forgiveness given by Christ? I say the Lord's Prayer nearly every day, including the sentence, "Forgive us our sins as we forgive those who sin against us." But I seem to have missed the point. I have said the words of forgiveness but not meant them. In this way, I have betrayed myself—and my God.

As I moved deeper into reflection, I became even more uncomfortable as I thought of myself as Judas. I suspect that most of us can recall times when we betrayed someone. The betrayals may have been deliberate or just thoughtless, but they happened nonetheless. We may have a complicated rationale for what we did, or failed to do, but sometimes we just dropped the ball or didn't realize the implications of our actions.

What's so compelling about this station is that all of us can relate to each role in this drama: betrayed and betrayer. And while it is helpful to review our lives, and acknowledge our mistakes, it is important to see the greater truths in this narrative. This is the strength and power of the Way of the Cross. It gives us insights into personal interactions and helps us see beyond our limited vision and understanding.

Shortly after I finished painting this station, I showed it to some friends. Deeply spiritual and sensitive people, they were clear that this painting was not simply about betrayal. This is about the arrest, they said. It is bigger than betrayal. It is about the world closing in on someone.

Often others will see something in a painting that I didn't even realize was there. This was no exception. The garden has been a place of refuge, a place where Jesus seeks comfort, but it suddenly becomes the site of the turning point in his journey. The arrest is the moment when the world takes over, and from here on, events cascade to his ultimate fate. We know how the story ends, that Jesus' fate is not what we might ordinarily expect— an important reminder when we feel as if our own world is closing in on us. But in the midst of the drama and pain, this is a difficult concept to hold on to.

I wonder about the vilification of Judas. After all, the hopeful ending to the Way of the Cross, the Resurrection, would never have happened unless the drama unfolded as it did. There needed to be a catalyst, something or someone who started the ball rolling. Judas was that catalyst. Just as we can never know the particulars or definite truth about Judas, we can never really know what happens in the heart of anyone else. It is difficult enough to understand ourselves and our own motivations, let alone those of another person. What is accomplished by focusing on others and their betrayal? How can we truly heal when we focus only on the hurt and pain caused by another?

This station shows us another way forward: to allow hurt and adversity help us transcend attachment to things of this world—our loved ones, culture, or comfort. Ultimately, this is our task—to see beyond this moment, this person, these circumstances, and to release our destiny to God. As I completed this chapter, I read these words, excerpts from a song, "Wash Your Spirit Clean" by the Native American group, Walela.

Be grateful for the struggle.
Be thankful for the lessons.
And you'll wash your spirit clean.
And you'll wash your spirit clean.

I   II   III   IV   V   VI   VII

PRAYER

" God of peace, help me to forgive those who hurt or betray me and strengthen me to be worthy of others' trust in me. Let your steadfast love and compassion flow through me that I may be your presence in this world. Help me to see beyond the pain of this moment to your divine plan. **Amen.** "

PETER DENIES JESUS III

"Simon, Simon, listen! Satan has demanded to sift all of you like wheat, but I have prayed for you that your own faith may not fail; and you, when once you have turned back, strengthen your brothers." And he said to him, "Lord, I am ready to go with you to prison and to death!" Jesus said, "I tell you, Peter, the cock will not crow this day, until you have denied three times that you know me."

– Luke 22:31-34

Throughout the gospels, there is a significant level of discomfort and denial any time Jesus speaks of his passion and death with his disciples. We can relate: no one wants to hear a beloved friend must die and suffer. Among the disciples, the most adverse and emotional reaction comes from Peter, who always seems to find it necessary to go a step further than anyone else in the group in order to demonstrate his undying fidelity and commitment to the Lord. It is Peter who declares Jesus to be "the Messiah, the Son of the living God" (Matthew 16:16).

As with any other human family and community, the disciples chosen by Jesus were a diverse and complex group of characters, to say the least. They too had to deal with the often-difficult temperaments of their colleagues, and there is little doubt that Peter is a fine example of what "difficult" and "hard-headed" can sometimes look like. He was also prone to use absolute terms that could get him into trouble: *Lord*, Peter says, *I would never deny you*.

Yet the cock crowed, just as the Lord had foretold. Surely it broke Peter's heart to hear that sound as he denied any association with his dearest friend for the third time. He must have been aware how his often-impulsive character had made him seem foolish and exaggeratedly emotional in the sight of the Lord and others. And of course, this time, the situation was much more than an impulsive act. This time, Peter issued a flat denial, abandoning his friend and Lord.

But we should not fall into the temptation of dumping all of this on Peter. There is a great deal of Peter in all of us, especially when we feel pressured and so often give in to life in ways that do not clearly identify us as followers of Jesus. This is especially evident in our contemporary Christian lives when we ignore or choose not to hear the cry of the poor, the hungry, the lonely, the discriminated, the undocumented, the rejected, and so many of those "little ones" Jesus invites us to receive, that are among us, and are still so neglected. It is then that the cock still crows.

FATHER ALBERTO R. CUTIÉ

DENIAL

Of all the stories of the Way of the Cross, this one is the most poignant to me. Even though I know what is coming and have read and thought about it many times, each time I hear the story again, the words are like a knife in my heart.

Jesus turns and looks at Peter. He doesn't scan the crowd, doesn't search for him among the faces in the darkness of pre-dawn; Jesus turns and looks directly at him. In my imagination, that look, that connection, is a moment frozen in time. Jesus looks into the eyes of Judas as he is betrayed. He sees his disciples and friends flee from him. And now with this denial, Jesus looks into Peter's eyes and knows he is utterly alone.

I suspect all of us have had the experience of denial, of holding out hope against hope that something terrible isn't really as bad as we think it might be. Then we experience the downward spiral, the crushing realization that it might be worse than we had imagined. Losing that last shred of hope is a wrenching moment. Things fall away as we realize that the old ways and old strategies don't work.

But then, sometimes, something else kicks in. An acceptance, a calm, a strength that comes from a depth we didn't know we had, a place we had never explored. Perhaps we reach this stage because we finally give up on our ability to solve or control things. We surrender, and in doing so, discover an exit from the dark basement that leads to a rich reservoir. Perhaps seeing his closest friend deny him was that moment for Jesus—the moment when he felt most alone, abandoned by friends, but also a recognition that God never leaves, that God is ever-present. The same is true for us: often situations that seem hopeless can open the door to God. We give up and let God in.

But what about Peter? What was that moment like for him? He was caught in a very difficult situation and was understandably confused and afraid. He was alone and vulnerable, and the consequences of aligning himself with Jesus could have been very serious. He loved Jesus, but he was afraid. I wonder if Peter even considered another option but to deny his friend. Try to see Peter with fresh eyes, as if you have never heard the story before. Imagine yourself with a close friend who is suddenly unjustly arrested and taken away. You are in enemy territory, you know no one, and you are essentially powerless. What would you do? How would you react? How much attention would you want drawn to yourself?

I know all too well my answers to these questions. I would deny Jesus and protect myself. Just like Peter. I know because I do this even today. Often those little denials sneak up on me and can seem so harmless. It may be something as simple as not saying anything when a conversation slips into malicious gossip—not wanting to be the wet blanket or to seem like I am moralizing. I deny Jesus when I start to criticize or gossip about someone else. I can always find a justification, "but it's true and talking about it isn't so harmful," but deep down, I know it is damaging and wrong. It's just so tempting to make myself feel better at someone else's expense, even though I know it doesn't really work that way. And in that moment, I deny that words can be hurtful,

and I fail to remember that some things are best left unsaid.

The denial continues when I recall the number of times I listened to people criticize my faith with stories and generalizations that are simply not accurate. Fortunately, I speak up more often about this now, in part because I have experienced the sting of turning my back on the truth for the sake of social acceptance or expedience.

Like Peter, when I deny my faith, when I get caught in the self and lose sight of the greater picture, I can't hide. Jesus is looking right at me. He sees me. And this is the humbling, amazing part: I am already forgiven. For my part, I must return the look. I must look into the eyes of Jesus and accept his compassion, love, and forgiveness.

This station is a defining moment for Jesus and for Peter. That look, the meeting of their eyes, holds eternity. The love of God transcends our concept of time and place and manifests beyond our ability to truly understand.

PRAYER

"Divine Friend, Fountain of Strength, give me courage to speak the truth and to stand for justice. When I fall short, help me accept your unfailing forgiveness and give me strength to continue, knowing that I am always in your sight. **Amen.**"

IV
THE CROWD CONDEMNS JESUS

Now Jesus stood before the governor; and the governor asked him, "Are you the King of the Jews?" Jesus said, "You say so."…While [Pilate] was sitting on the judgment seat, his wife sent word to him, "Have nothing to do with that innocent man, for today I have suffered a great deal because of a dream about him." Now the chief priests and the elders persuaded the crowds to ask for Barabbas and to have Jesus killed. The governor again said to them, "Which of the two do you want me to release for you?" And they said, "Barabbas." Pilate said to them, "Then what should I do with Jesus who is called the Messiah?" All of them said, "Let him be crucified!" Then he asked, "Why, what evil has he done?" But they shouted all the more, "Let him be crucified!" So when Pilate saw that he could do nothing, but rather that a riot was beginning, he took some water and washed his hands before the crowd, saying, "I am innocent of this man's blood; see to it yourselves." Then the people as a whole answered, "His blood be on us and on our children!" So he released Barabbas for them; and after flogging Jesus, he handed him over to be crucified.

– Matthew 27:11-26

Peter, in fear, has denied Jesus, and now so does Pilate. Ignoring his wife's admonishment that Jesus is innocent, and his own astute political intuition that the authorities who have handed Jesus over to him have dubious motives. Ignoring what he himself knows to be right, Pilate chooses not do the good that is in his power to do.

Jesus has been handed over to him, and Pilate has the power to decide. He has power, even though he tells himself that there is nothing he can do. He has power to make a difference in the life of the one who now stands before him. Pilate must choose, and act, and live with the consequences of that action. The one who will be Judge of All is judged by Pilate, and the basic question Pilate must answer is one that every soul must decide: Who is this man, and what will be my response to him?

The central image here is of a pair of hands. The washing of hands is a delusion. Pilate protests that he is innocent of Jesus' blood, but he is not—as none of us are. There is no escaping the responsibility. Jesus is in his hands. And ours.

Pilate's hand-washing is really just a hand-wringing, after too easy an abdication. It is the picture of a soul refusing to bear responsibility for its decisions. Refusing to aid, or to share in the sufferings of another. And so the one with power to decide, and to act, and to make a difference becomes yet another guilty bystander.

Pilate washes his hands to transfer onto others responsibility for a choice that he has made. But in truth, he cannot do this. In the same way, the soul senses a need to be cleansed, senses that it is caught in a network of compromises and evasions and avoidances, sees in itself the fruit of that fear that blocks true compassion. The decisions that result are ours—our responsibility and ours alone—but we need help to deal with them. We need a savior.

But Pilate washes his hands, and hands Jesus over. Jesus, who stood up for the outcast, embraced the sinner, and ministered God's love to all. In Jesus' time of need, Pilate does not raise a helping hand higher than the basin he has had brought to him. Pilate in us is no different.

In Christ, we can be different. In the light of Christ, we can see our way to make a difference. And we can learn to ask, as we look out from our places of power and privilege: Who is this who has been handed over to us? Into our hands? What will be our response, our decision? A futile hand-washing? Or a taking by the hand, our hands extended to help?

BISHOP BARRY BEISNER

I   II   III   IV   V   VI   VII

JUDGMENT

Aside from the brutality and injustice in this passage, something has always puzzled me. Did Pilate really think he could simply wash his hands of the matter and claim innocence, in spite of his ultimate power over Jesus' fate?

Pilate had a history and a reputation of being crafty and ruthless. Although scripture doesn't tell us much about Pilate's life before he presides at Jesus' trial, ancient Jewish writers describe Pilate as vindictive, inflexible, and relentless.

In some ways, this past makes it all the more puzzling that Pilate gives the audience the power over Jesus' fate. But we also know that this is not just the trial of any Jew, the unfortunate story of one man. Pilate's wife even suffers "a great deal" because of her dream about Jesus. Something was moving deep in the collective unconscious. Clearly this trial was beyond the normal routine of the Roman courts. Pilate seems to have known that.

In allowing the crowd to choose who should live and who should die, Pilate abdicates his duty. He even goes so far as to physically wash his hands of the matter. This action brings to mind the water of baptism, which symbolically cleanses new Christians and marks a new beginning. So does Pilate's decision. The decision to give up control and let the crowd choose marks a turning point in the narrative. We witness Jesus' betrayal at every level, by his friends, the Jewish community, and the Roman courts. From this point on, the story will unfold without influence or interference of other people. Now begins the long walk to Calvary. Pilate washing his hands symbolizes the release of Jesus' destiny from any earthly power or influence.

Because we know the rest of the story, Jesus' death and resurrection, it is impossible to imagine that the story could play out any other way. Yet I wonder what would have happened if Pilate taken responsibility for the decision. Would he have listened to the voice of his wife warning him to have nothing to do with Jesus? What would have happened if even one person had spoken up in the face of this injustice?

I think we have all had the experience of watching something terrible unfold and feeling powerless to do anything about it. But how often are we really hiding behind fear? Or, like Pilate, claiming there is nothing more we can do? I worry about our current culture as I watch the level of civility drop around me. Language becomes increasingly coarse, pornography and violence become mainstream, and at times, it seems that no one else even seems to notice.

It's tempting to think that outside of making personal decisions about my own behavior and attitudes, I have little power to do anything about it. The culture has its own trajectory, and I can only do what I believe to be right. Yet, in truth there are things that I can do, statements I can make, stands I can take. Am I holding back because I am afraid to be labeled as a prude? Am I afraid to go against the tide? Am I hiding behind excuses, trying to wash my hands of whatever influence I might have? Am I Pilate?

PRAYER

"Gracious God, be with me in all adversity. Give me strength and wisdom to do your will. May I always put my faith in your ultimate truth and my hope in your enduring grace. **Amen.**"

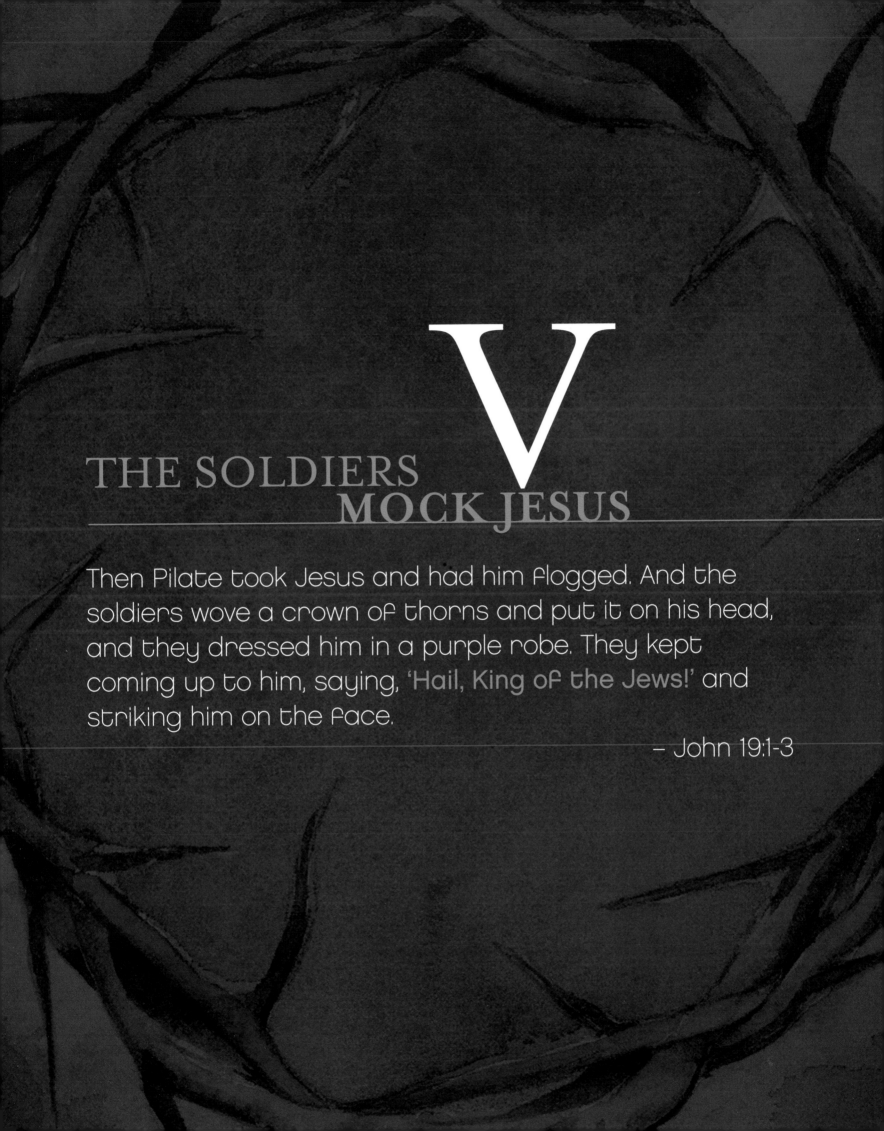

V

THE SOLDIERS MOCK JESUS

Then Pilate took Jesus and had him flogged. And the soldiers wove a crown of thorns and put it on his head, and they dressed him in a purple robe. They kept coming up to him, saying, 'Hail, King of the Jews!' and striking him on the face.

— John 19:1-3

The Stations of the Cross had not been a significant part of my devotional life, especially the ones that are painfully realistic. When Kathrin began working on the stations, I wasn't interested until I saw that she was doing an impressionistic representation in which Jesus, the Holy One, was depicted as light. I saw this station early in her process and was immediately moved by it. It seemed to draw me into the story and beyond it.

The crown of thorns is a powerful symbol. I try to imagine what the soldiers were doing and thinking as they were making it. Why make it of thorns? Was that the easiest material to find? Perhaps so. But thorns are difficult to work with and must have caused some pain in making it. Were the soldiers thinking about making a crown that might inflict as much pain as possible? Were they just following orders? Or was this crown of thorns their idea, their contribution to the Crucifixion? The crown is a powerful symbol of both royalty and divinity. Did they realize the full implications of what they were doing?

This representation of the crown with its wicked thorns anchors us not only in the painful reality of the situation in which Jesus was caught, but it also immediately draws us into the immensity of the reality beyond it—into God's divine energy of love that fills the universe. We are not alone, caught on the thorns of difficult or humiliating situations. God's light of love surrounds us, upholds us, and draws us into its center to sustain us and to lift us beyond the thorns so that we may be empowered to deal with these situations as best we can. That divine light that we see through the window of the thorns draws us ever beyond ourselves into the dazzling mystery of love.

I wonder if the soldiers who created that crown were touched by the power and intensity of that love and presence, even as they attempted to torture him? I think they must have been.

SISTER TERESA MARIE MARTIN

HUMILIATION

I completed this painting first. I had experimented with various approaches— figurative, narrative, abstract—but none seemed to click. It just didn't feel right to work with specific figures or images, since the real power of the story was the way it touches each of us in the here and now.

In this particular station, I knew the depiction of individuals would be a distraction. But I needed a recognizable image. I wanted to find the essence of each station, the part that speaks to each of us personally. Quite honestly, I was a little surprised that this station, which at first glance seemed the most difficult, would open that door. But then, this experience expresses what the Way of the Cross is about—a passage to another reality.

I find inspiration for art in unexpected places. One might think that inspiration is only found in great works of art, famous historical sites, or profound experiences. More often than not, the mundane or common holds the most gold for me. Many years ago, my husband and I were traveling in France and stopped at

a small gallery in a village in Brittany where a student was exhibiting oil paintings. They were fairly primitive paintings done on bed sheets—an economical way to paint but not a medium with a lot of archival promise. The paintings were obviously beginning attempts of a young artist, but they had life and energy. One of the paintings that really spoke to me showed ladders leaning against the sky, going up to doorways. It was simple, but the concept resonated with me.

I loved the idea of punching a hole in the sky, of going to another reality. I confess that I stole the idea and have played with it in my own work for many years. In fact, I even have a two-foot-long ladder leaning against the wall of my studio. To some, it might seem like kitsch or junk, but to me it is an invitation to go beyond, to enter another place, which is really at the heart of my art and my faith.

As the passage tells us, Jesus is at the mercy of his captors. Bit by bit, his support has fallen away, until he is the object of derision and hatred. Even more, he is humiliated by the soldiers who force him to wear a crown of thorns—a distorted and cruel mockery for an innocent man.

Of all the elements of this part of the story, I began to focus on the crown of thorns. We generally think of crowns as beautiful objects made of precious materials—gold, studded with diamonds or other precious gemstones. But in this case, the crown of thorns is the exact opposite. Thorns are earthy and dangerous. We speak of someone as a thorn in our side, or we find ourselves in a thorny situation. For Jesus, the crown of thorns was an excruciating prelude to torture and his eventual Crucifixion.

A crown also symbolizes a link between the individual and the divine, between heaven and earth. Royalty wear crowns because of the traditional belief that they are close to divine, or even divine themselves. The crown represents the connection between the wearer and God. In looking at the body through a metaphysical lens, the top of head, or seventh chakra, is called the crown—a link to the divine.

The crown of thorns symbolizes another step in the transformation of Jesus. While the crown connects Jesus to the earth through the thorns, it is also a connection with the divine. Jesus is on the path to death and resurrection, to being at the right hand of God the Father. While we likely won't ever wear a crown of thorns, we can relate to the transforming power of pain and humiliation. Often the difficulties of life serve as catalysts that force us to move out of our ego and to face the world from a deeper and wider place in our hearts. When we are brought to that place where we think we have no choices left, we often realize that the one right choice was there all along— the choice of surrender to God. And when we are willing to do that, the world beyond opens up for us. As John Peterson states so well in his book, *A Walk in Jerusalem*, this is the "Divine Reversal," the first sign that through Jesus, God is going to turn everything upside down.

We often hear of people who have been grateful for a life-threatening disease, or a close encounter with death. A friend told me of her experience when she was a young mother. She was not yet thirty years old, with three small children, when she discovered that she had breast cancer. This was in the 1970s when cancer treatment was still experimental and the prognosis was not good. Her husband, unable to cope with the stress and pain, abandoned the family. She was on her own, alone, and frightened. The odds of her survival were slim. Fortunately, she survived the cancer and went on to raise her family and live a full and creative life. Now in her sixties, she doesn't look back to those frightening times with anger or bitterness. She sees them as a time when God turned everything upside down for her and her children. Before the diagnosis, she was living a life of relative ease, taking things for granted, and not paying much attention to God. She was the center of her own comfortable universe. Finding herself alone in a difficult position, with an uncertain future, forced her to see that things were not as she had believed. Another reality opened up for her, and she saw things from a different perspective, one that did not have her immediate concerns at its core. As is so often the case, the pain and challenges of life opened a window to another reality.

I   III   IV   V   VI   VII

PRAYER

"Merciful God, be with me in times of humiliation and despair. Give me hope, and let me know that I am always worthy in your sight. Clothe me in your love. **Amen.**"

JESUS CARRIES HIS CROSS

VI

And carrying the cross by himself, he went out to the Place of the Skull, which in Hebrew is called Golgotha.

— John 19:17

In the swirling drama that is the Passion of Our Lord Jesus Christ, many things leap out at the reader. Chief among them must surely be the cross itself, the means by which the savior of the world was executed. As if the cross itself is not shocking enough, Jesus was forced to carry his own cross to the execution site. Being fully human, Jesus must have found this not only physically challenging but also emotionally devastating.

Poets look at the cross and see the intersection of heaven and earth—the horizontal beam representing humanity, and the vertical beam indicating our relationship with God. But it must not have seemed poetic to the man who had to carry the heavy wooden device on which he would die.

And what of the place? Golgotha. The Place of the Skull, so named perhaps because so many skeletons of the deceased were seen there. It was a desolate place. Today, in Jerusalem's Church of the Holy Sepulchre, it is possible to see and to touch a stone outcropping that tradition tells us is the precise site where Jesus was crucified. The stone is just as you'd expect: unforgiving, brutally hard, and mercilessly gray.

Popular culture might have us focus on the nails by which Jesus was hanged on the cross. But the ancient church was more interested in the "hard wood of the Cross, on which hung the savior of the world." The earliest Christians were awed and horrified not just by iron, but by stone and wood. To leap from the world of stone, iron, and wood to the world of flesh, warmth, and perfect love is to cross an uncrossable chasm.

And that, my friends, is the mystery of the Passion. God's perfect love was rejected by the world. We surely know how this is part of the arc of God's plan of salvation for the world, but this knowledge does not diminish our sorrow for Christ's death and for the desolation of humanity. How could we do this?

Here we can rest assured that just as God's love is stronger than death, God's love can redeem us. God's love is stronger than our fears. The painting here gets it right. A worldly, horrific cross stands before us. Just beyond, still in our sight, is the light of God's love. The cross is not just a gruesome object. The cross is our promise of God's love, despite all odds.

FATHER SCOTT GUNN

I   II   III   IV   V   VI   VII

SUFFERING

Several years ago I participated in Education for Ministry, a four-year theological study program developed by Sewanee: The University of the South, a seminary of The Episcopal Church. The readings and discussions cover the Old and New Testaments, church history, and theology.

The program leads participants into a deeper understanding of the Christian faith and also touches on other paths as well. During one discussion, I remarked that I was struck by the emphasis on suffering in the Buddhist faith. One of the other participants looked at me like I was crazy and said, "What do you think the cross is about in Christianity?" Indeed. It was a good question, or more accurately, a good point. As we witness Jesus carrying the instrument of his impending death, we cannot help but see the cross as a sign of suffering. We can also understand the cross as a symbol that applies to our own individual lives. Disappointment, problems, and pain are the stuff of life. And while not pleasant, they provide grist for the mill and opportunities for growth.

We all have crosses to bear. One of my favorite anecdotes is a story of a young Texas socialite back in the 1960s who was complaining to her maid about being overwhelmed. I think she was grumbling about the Junior League and the demands that it made on her time and energy. The maid listened patiently for as long as she could, and then said, "Honey, we all got our crosses to bear. You've got the Junior League, and I've got you."

It's always something. It might be something that is irritating—a friend or family member who drives us crazy. Or it might be more serious or debilitating than that—a physical disability or health problem that impacts our life. Or, it might be an impulsive decision that changes our course and keeps us from living the life we thought we would have. Whatever it is, it is ours to carry and ours to resolve. And this is the important part—it is an essential part of our journey.

The cross symbolizes more than the burdens we bear. Viewed metaphorically, the horizontal and the vertical bars each represent a different facet of our human nature. The horizontal is the physical in the here and now (or what we believe to be the here and now). It signifies our physical being and our connection with one another and all of creation. It speaks to the interconnectedness of all that exists on the earthly plane. It points to our need for community and for relationship with one other. The vertical arm of the cross is a sign of our link with the Divine, the connection between our temporal existence (which we sometimes perceive to be reality) and the ultimate reality that lies in eternity.

The cross represents a true and abiding link between ourselves and God, between the earthly existence and the eternal. It shows us that through Christ, the two realities intersect.

That intersection is where we enter the Way, the path toward wisdom. The experiences of life and community—the trials, the pain, and the suffering, as well as the joys and triumphs—are all part of the journey. At the same time, we seek, and sometimes find, the greater eternal reality. We do not exist simply to suffer and deal with hardships. Nor are we exempt from the trials of life, regardless of how deep our faith. Each part of our being and experience informs the other. We grow toward greater understanding and closeness to God to the extent that we are willing to live life fully, carry our burdens, and consciously deal with difficulties.

The central image in this station was obvious. I had already decided that images of faces and figures would be a distraction. And the cross is a straightforward archetypal image. But at the same time, the cross is such a common image that its power can be diminished by its familiarity and its message overlooked. I wanted the cross to be seen with new eyes. Above the cross, I painted a dark indigo of eternity, below, the green of the earth—two realities that sometimes seem at odds and incompatible. The cross unites these complementary parts of our being as well. But unless we take up our own cross and enter the Way, the cross remains merely a symbol. The cross is tipped slightly so that the image would be more active, for it doesn't describe one moment or one single event. It describes a way, the Way, which is a journey and progression.

Life is not static. Our problems are not static. There is always movement in one direction or another. Jesus willingly took up his cross, and we are called to do the same.

"Wanderer, your footsteps are the road, and nothing more; wanderer, there is no road, the road is made by walking. By walking one makes the road, and upon glancing behind one sees the path that never will be trod again. Wanderer, there is no road—Only wakes upon the sea."

Antonio Machado,
Campos de Castilla, 1912

PRAYER

"Almighty God, help me to accept and understand the pain and hardships of this life. Give me strength to meet my challenges and bear my burdens. Grant me grace to grow in holiness, and the will to take up my cross and follow you. **Amen.**"

VI

SIMON OF CYRENE
ASSISTS JESUS

They compelled a passer-by, who was coming in from the country, to carry his cross: it was Simon of Cyren the father of Alexander and Rufus.

– Mark 15

We know very little about Simon of Cyrene. Various legends have arisen around Simon, but the scriptures say precious little. Matthew, Mark, and Luke all agree that Simon was compelled to carry the cross for Jesus. Why is this act recorded in all three Passion narratives?

The scene when Jesus was carrying the cross to Golgotha must have been horrific. Jesus' followers, at least those who had the courage to be nearby, must have watched with a mixture of sorrow, outrage, and disbelief. How could this be happening? How could their leader, the Messiah, be facing this humiliating and agonizing death? Where is the redemption amid shame and suffering? For modern readers to soften this encounter would be to look away from the very depths of the Passion.

If we take the gospels at face value, Simon was compelled to bear the cross. That is, he did not do this willingly. He was, the passion narratives tell us, a mere passerby. And yet it fell to him to carry the cross on which Jesus would be killed. This must have been painful and perhaps even embarrassing. So what can we learn from this? Where is the redemption?

Jesus again and again tells his followers that they must take up their cross and follow him. Simon—who may or may not have been a follower of Jesus—literally took up Jesus' cross and walked with him. Most of us, thanks be to God, never will be asked to make this kind of sacrifice, to literally take up a cross.

But we Christians are called to take up the burdens of others. Sometimes we will be compelled to do this, whether or not we want to. Where is the redemption?

When we take up the burdens of another, we can do this knowing that Christ walks with us. When we carry the burdens of another, we can see that the burden of another is eased. We can take up the cross knowing that God is near. In this is redemption.

FATHER SCOTT GUNN

HELP

One of the blessings of painting the Way of the Cross is that the project forced me to spend time with scripture in deeper ways than I ever had. I had done some study of scripture, including a method called *lectio divina*, and found it to be very helpful in terms of entering the story and making it personal.

But staying with the Way of the Cross for many months made me read, reread, and sometimes reconsider a story that I thought I knew pretty well. I often read too quickly and miss obvious details, or see it in my mind's eye the way I think it should be, rather than what is written. What I discovered about this station surprised me. As described in just one sentence in each of the synoptic gospels, Simon was a passerby who was enlisted to carry the cross for Jesus. I had never imagined it this way. In my mind, Simon helped Jesus carry the cross. Yet it is clear in scripture that Simon carried the cross for Jesus. This puts a whole new spin on the story for me. How does something we never asked for become our cross to bear?

This station reminds me that we all have crosses to bear, and more importantly, these crosses all relate to our walk with Christ. This takes my problems, my pains, and my disappointments and puts them in a new perspective. In shouldering the burden and taking responsibility, I am walking the Way. I'm not saying that we're always called to take on others' burdens but rather that we should not live life simply as an observer. This deep involvement in life—our own and that of others—gives us meaning and moves us closer to God.

A good friend of mine, Sister Teresa, is a remarkable woman of many talents (including as a contributor to this book). Currently serving as the superior of the Community of the Transfiguration of which I am an associate, she amazes me with the breadth and depth of her interests and knowledge. When she gets interested in a subject, she dives in and learns about it with single-mindedness and enthusiasm. J.R.R. Tolkien's great series, *The Lord of the Rings*, is one of her passions. She has read the books and seen the movies many times and even gives workshops on the Christian approach to the works. When she first saw the painting for this station, the two hands clasped in front of the cross, she said it reminded her of images in two of the films of *The Lord of the Rings*. I hadn't recalled those scenes, so I went back to find them.

The first instance is near the end of *The Fellowship of the Ring* when Frodo, the main character, wants to protect his friend and decides to make the journey alone. But committed to his friend, Sam dives into the water after him. As Sam flails in the water, beginning to drown, Frodo reaches down and pulls Sam up into the boat with him. The image of the two hands clasping beneath the water is a powerful illustration of friendship and devotion.

The second image is from the third film, *The Return of the King*, when Frodo is wrestling with Gollum, an enemy, on the edge of a precipice above a deadly inferno. Frodo slips and is about to go over the edge when Sam, who has been hiding, runs to him, extends his hand and pulls him up.

The reaching hand of help, in both cases a life-saving clasp, has gone both ways. Frodo saved Sam from drowning and Sam saved Frodo from falling to his death in the fire. And so it is with Christ. He reaches to us, just as we reach out to him. Simon the Helper is each

of us. We may be minding our own business when we're called off of the street, a passerby asked to carry a cross; this encounter with Christ, that helping hand, can turn a life around.

Nancy was one of the members of my Education for Ministry program. Over the course of her life, she has worked in science and engineering and recently earned her law degree. She's involved with her local church and with the diocese. Nevertheless, at one of our meetings, Nancy wondered aloud what her ministry might be, how she might contribute to the church and to the world. Her remark was met with stunned silence. We were a bit dumbfounded. Here was a marvelous example of someone using her many gifts to help and bless people, both within and outside of the church. She is truly living her ministry, so intrinsically in fact, that she doesn't even know that she is doing it. Finally, someone said, "Nancy, you are living your ministry. That is what it is all about." And the light bulb seemed to go on.

Simon just happened to be passing by. Nancy just happened to be practicing law when the new nonprofit organization needed help, or the small rural church needed guidance. She just happens to be available to bless the Taizé community with the heavenly sounds of her flute. She just happens to offer pastoral care and comfort to patients in the local hospital.

Like Nancy and Simon, we are called from *where* we are to be *who* we are in our walk with Christ. The more readily we respond, and the more fully that we are ourselves, the more we serve Christ and live out our ministry in the Way.

VIII

JESUS MEETS THE WOMEN OF JERUSALEM

A great number of the people followed him, and among them were women who were beating their breasts and wailing for him. But Jesus turned to them and said, "Daughters of Jerusalem, do not weep for me, but weep for yourselves and for your children. For the days are surely coming when they will say, 'Blessed are the barren, and the wombs that never bore, and the breasts that never nursed.' Then they will begin to say to the mountains, 'Fall on us'; and to the hills, 'Cover us.' For if they do this when the wood is green, what will happen when it is dry?"

– Luke 23:27-31

The road into Jerusalem is bustling on this sultry midmorning as the crowds jostle into the city to buy provisions for the evening's solemn meal. An official procession of Roman soldiers, temple police, religious officials, and curious onlookers makes its way in the opposite direction. Within this procession are three men on their way to be crucified on a rocky outcropping outside the city gate. Caught in the cross-traffic are a good number of followers of one of the men condemned to death. Among the followers is a band of women clutching their children, scanning the procession for their leader.

A warm, moist wind whips up a cloud of dust, and when it clears, they see their beloved teacher, pulled and prodded by the soldiers. The women gather the children under their mantles to shield them from the horrible sight. These grief-stricken women beat their breasts, letting out anguished cries. Jesus strains to turn toward the women, and their eyes meet his. Words struggle to form on his parched and torn lips as he utters these words in Luke that echo down through the centuries and fall even now on my ears.

Jesus, may I have the courage to go against the flow of the crowd and let me never turn away from seeing your face in the innocent who suffer pain and anguish as a result of unjust systems.

Could there be such a catastrophe that would cause a mother to regret having brought a new life into this world? Spare me from ever having to face such a day, and never let me fail to find joy in the miracle of new life no matter how troubled the circumstances. Open my heart also to reverence those who are not able, or consciously choose not, to bear children of their own, and those, who out of unselfish love, parent, in various ways, the children of others.

Jesus, give me the fortitude never to hide in the face of tragedy but to do what is in my power to mitigate the sufferings of others; and when nothing else can be done, give me the patience to be present with them, and let me never turn away from their suffering.

Never allow me to be seduced by the deceiver into thinking that I can live unto myself and apart from you. To do that is to choose my own destruction. In all of my own pains, may I never become so self-absorbed as to miss an opportunity to express compassion in the suffering of others.

May I learn from you, my all-loving Jesus, the redemptive work of compassion for the healing and well-being of the whole creation.

FRIAR LEO M. JOSEPH

PRAYER

"Divine Helper, may I be the hand of Christ, reaching out to help those in need. Make me an instrument of your peace and a messenger of your loving kindness. **Amen.**"

VIII   IX   X   XI   XII   XIII   XIV

WITNESS

For as long as I can remember, I have created artwork in series. Many years ago when I was a potter, I would throw a run of similar bowls until I had a hundred or more. Same with mugs or any other vessel I was creating. When I started painting, I continued the practice.

An image or a concept intrigues me, and I stay with it over a series of paintings, sometimes for years. I find that in this way I can enter into the deeper meaning of an image and explore it at an unconscious level. Very often, I don't even put words or descriptions to the paintings until well into or even after the series is complete. That is how it was with the Way of the Cross. I started with words, by studying the scriptures, reading commentary and doing *lectio divina* as preparation. But when I started painting, I tried to step aside and allow the images to come from a nonverbal place.

Earlier in my career, I painted a series of frogs for about five years. As the work became known, I heard from wildlife biologists and environmental activists who wondered if the inspiration for the work was the possible extinction of frogs and other amphibians. While I found that decline to be troubling, I told them my focus in the work was not primarily biological or environmental, but spiritual and symbolic. In most of those paintings, the frog was generally the witness, quietly regarding nature—a sunrise, sunset, or a burst of light behind a water lily. But since people were curious, I was compelled to look into the symbolism a little deeper. The frog is an animal that lives both in water and land. It can live in two realms, and in fact, needs both in order to survive. It is no coincidence that frogs feature prominently in fairy tales and mythology. They are a strong archetypal image of the dual nature of humankind. Going a bit farther with this metaphor, the frog represents complementary parts of ourselves that we need to acknowledge and honor in order to become realized and fully human—the conscious and the unconscious, the physical and spiritual.

For spiritual growth, we need a witness—an inner observer. This is what we cultivate in contemplative prayer—one who watches our machinations, hears our inner dialogues and chatter, but yet is somehow outside of the personal drama. In a sense, this observer is a bridge between God and our selves and exists at the point of the cross where the two beams meet. This is where our soul resides and touches both realities. In this image, the women, the feminine, symbolize the witness. They are onlookers who are emotionally involved and grieve for Jesus. Yet Jesus tells them. "Do not weep for me. Weep for yourselves and your children." He is making it clear that the Way is not primarily about his suffering—we are not to view the crucifixion as merely a painful drama of man's cruelty to man. That is of course a component, and our emotional response and compassion are part of the experience. However, we are not merely onlookers. If we refuse to see this experience as our own story, we miss the greater point.

The Way of the Cross is much more than a moving story; it shows us the path to God. It shows us that suffering is part of life and that no one is exempt from pain. At the same time, we are called to have compassion and love for others, especially in the midst of their hardships.

In his remarkable book, *Man's Search for Meaning*, Victor Frankl describes his experiences in the Auschwitz concentration camp and how he was able to survive such dehumanizing and cruel circumstances. It was the thought of something greater, something beyond those horrible experiences that gave him the strength to carry on. He learned that believing in something beyond himself, something beyond pain, can give purpose and the will to survive. The pain and suffering do not go away but are transformed into deeper understanding, compassion for others, and an acceptance of our responsibility to do what is right.

The women were not to weep for Jesus but for themselves and their loved ones. Jesus admonishes them to apply the story to their own lives—to understand that his experience is the experience of each of us. Jesus knew that this was not the totality of his experience; that what would happen next was bigger than than any of them could realize. Yet he did not give the distraught women words of comfort, but rather a challenge. So too today, Jesus challenges each of us to open our eyes and hearts to the pain and hardship around us, and through our faith and actions, respond with God's abiding love.

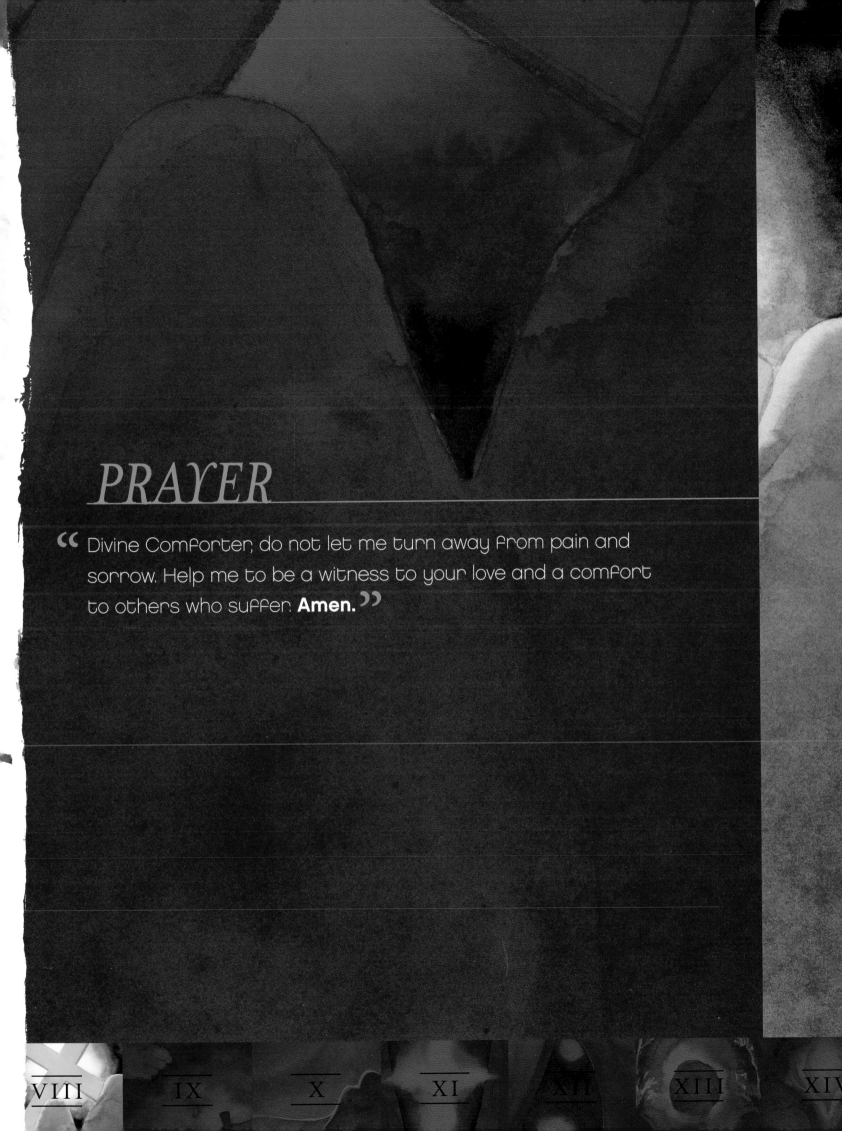

PRAYER

" Divine Comforter, do not let me turn away from pain and sorrow. Help me to be a witness to your love and a comfort to others who suffer. **Amen.** "

IX

SOLDIERS NAIL
JESUS TO THE CROSS

Then they brought Jesus to the place called Golgotha
(which means the place of a skull). And they offered
him wine mixed with myrrh; but he did not take it.
And they crucified him, and divided his clothes among
them, casting lots to decide what each should take.
It was nine o'clock in the morning when they crucified
him. The inscription of the charge against him read,
"The King of the Jews."

– Mark 15:22-26

I hear, O Jesus, the sound of the hammer blows as they drive the crude iron nails into the soft flesh between your wrist bones and then into the ligaments of the rough timber cross. As the point of the nails pass through to the bare rock beneath the wood, the metallic sound reverberates as if it could split the very earth to its molten core, as indeed it pierces your mother, Mary, to the core of her being. The soldier's task is swiftly done, as with his ruddy woolen mantel John tries to shield Mary from the horror.

Now the crossbeam is hoisted in place on top of the upright post, and the final nail is quickly driven through your feet, securing your ultimate loss of physical freedom.

Final loss of liberty comes to us all, O Jesus, whether sick bed or deathbed, imposed or chosen, the prison or the monastic cell, old age or youthful tragedy, when suddenly or gradually, we are deprived of our physical freedom and our material world, left only to exist in the interior realm.

O Jesus, in these, my dying days, help me to forgive all who in any way have added to my burden of pain and have pointed the finger of blame and heaped shame on me. Give me the courage and love to let go of all the bitter and noxious thoughts and every evil intention against those who have done harm to me or have abandoned me in my time of need.

To fulfill the scripture, your executioners divided your clothes among themselves. As you endured the spoiling of your possessions, enable me to dispose of my material goods according to your will. Teach me to keep a light grasp on all things and to discern what is appropriate and helpful according to my current circumstances, holding on to nothing that can take hold of me.

When those who love me draw near in my waning days, give me the grace not to turn them away in my selfishness but to reach out to them for the love and support that I will need. Give me the care and wisdom to provide for my loved ones when I am no longer able to do so, and to so order my affairs that our common bonds of love may endure long after my last breath. Jesus, in spite of loss of movement, enable me to love and to know that love's labor continues until the last heartbeat.

In my final struggle, grant me the honesty to cry out with you in utter abandonment the words of Psalm 22 that you prayed, *"My God, my God, why have you forsaken me? and are so far from my cry and from the words of my distress? And the endurance to breathe forth my spirit with the psalm's closing words, Praise the LORD, you that fear him; stand in awe of him, O offspring of Israel; all you of Jacob's line, give glory."*

The Book of Common Prayer

FRIAR LEO M. JOSEPH

I   II   III   IV   V   VI   VII

SURRENDER

Jesus is nailed to the cross. The path has become increasingly inhumane and cruel. We have gone from betrayal and abandonment to this, the unthinkable torture of a brutal murder.

In each of our lives, there is the moment when we realize that we cannot escape the cross that is ours to bear. The drama of each life plays out as it will. Life throws us curves, challenges, disappointments, even tragedy, and at some point we must face it alone. Someone once pointed out that we all die alone, regardless of how many people are gathered at the bedside. As the Way shows us, in order to transcend the limitations of our usual understanding, we must surrender. We must be willing to lose everything in order to gain that which is most precious. "Those who find their life will lose it, and those who lose their life for my sake will find it" Mathew 10:39.

Even on the cross, Jesus petitions on our behalf: "Father, forgive them, for they do not know what they are doing." Jesus understands us; he knows our limitations. We are human, after all. He sees us through the eternal eyes of compassion, understanding, and acceptance. This is the way to the cross and to transcendence.

The Crucifixion itself is described in three words: "they crucified him." This simple sentence does not express the outrageous pain and agony that Jesus is experiencing, so it is easy to gloss over the enormity of his suffering. Later, at his death, he will become completely merged with the Other and freed from the bonds of the physical, but at this point, Jesus is enduring unimaginable pain. Yet, he lives in forgiveness.

This is an example of Jesus' ultimate acceptance. Through his example, we can learn to accept those things, however painful, that we cannot change. The first part of the *Serenity Prayer*, commonly attributed to Reinhold Niebuhr, is familiar to most as a key tool of many Twelve Step programs: "God, grant me the serenity to accept the things I cannot change;

courage to change the things I can; and wisdom to know the difference." But the lesser-known second part takes us even closer to the heart of surrender:"Living one day at a time; enjoying one moment at a time; accepting hardships as the pathway to peace. Taking, as [God] did, this sinful world as it is, not as I would have it; trusting that he will make all things right if I surrender to his will; that I may be reasonably happy in this life and supremely happy with him forever in the next."

Another example of this type of acceptance is the Welcoming Prayer, found in the tradition of Centering Prayer. With this technique, we accept and welcome our burdens, especially those we create ourselves. Rather than resisting, we welcome self-criticism, fear, anxiety, or whatever might be attaching to us and causing suffering. Paradoxically, this welcoming of suffering transforms the pain and energy and opens the door to another reality. Once we move through this door, the threat subsides: we have extinguished its power by refusing to struggle or resist.

When I first learned the technique in Welcoming Prayer, I was skeptical. After all, I had cultivated these inner dialogues and battles for a lifetime; I was pretty good at wrestling with that inner voice that regularly tormented me with doubt, fear, and worry. I began to realize that each time I engaged with and fought against the inner voices of criticism, I gave those fears more energy. So I was reluctant at first to embrace Welcoming Prayer. It seemed too easy to say, "Welcome fear, come on in!" Then poof! It would vanish. Just like that. But it worked. To my amazement, it still works.

Voicing these worries and self-doubts, welcoming them into the light of day, strips them of their dark power. It allows me to put my trust where it belongs: with God.

Jesus' example of surrender is the exemplar. He does not struggle or condemn. He even asks forgiveness for his executors. He accepts and forgives. And just as he loves and accepts us, we are called to love and accept one another and perhaps more challenging, to love and accept ourselves. When we surrender, we experience Christ's unconditional love and acceptance.

When we accept the things we cannot change, we grow closer to God. As Saint Francis said, "It is in dying that we are reborn into eternal life."

PRAYER

" Eternal God, give me strength to endure pain and injustice. Comfort me when I am overwhelmed and do not turn your face from my distress. **Amen.** "

X

MARY AND THE BELOVED DISCIPLE STAND AT THE FOOT OF THE CROSS

Meanwhile, standing near the cross of Jesus were his mother, and his mother's sister, Mary the wife of Clopas, and Mary Magdalene. When Jesus saw his mother and the disciple whom he loved standing beside her, he said to his mother, "Woman, here is your son." Then he said to the disciple, "Here is your mother." And from that hour the disciple took her into his own home.

– John 19:25-27

As a young adult, I experienced the entire process of death, as my seemingly very healthy middle-aged father was diagnosed with cancer, became ill, and eventually died. Those experiences and the very traumatic process of mourning were undoubtedly painful, yet they taught me many valuable lessons. I learned that most people run away from the cross. Very few friends will stick around for the most difficult moments.

Throughout our lives, we all have our moments on the cross, when we find ourselves in an immense amount of physical, spiritual, or emotional suffering. At other moments, we are invited by the circumstances of life to be at the "Foot of the Cross," accompanying friends and loved ones in difficulties. As we contemplate the cross, we see the power of love and the importance of Christian community. We are reminded that we are not alone in this world and maybe that is why Jesus himself— the Word made flesh—chose and formed a community of believers, the spiritual family we call church.

One of the most touching moments in the Sunday Eucharist is when we, the community, arrive at the Prayers of the People. After formal petitions are read, *The Book of Common Prayer* instructs us that "the people may add their own petitions." If you pay close attention, you'll hear the whispers of names, petitions, thanksgivings, and a variety of prayers, as well as the names of people who may not be physically present but are surely spiritually remembered and united through prayer. At that moment, you can witness the Christian community at the "Foot of the Cross," gazing upon the crucified and the suffering they have encountered in their lives and relationships. It is a powerful moment of prayer, for we realize that we are all connected and united, that a spiritual family of sisters and brothers has been brought together at the "Foot of the Cross" of our humanity.

FATHER ALBERTO R. CUTIÉ

COMPASSION

While researching the tradition of the Stations of the Cross, I learned of at least nineteen stations. The use of fourteen is fairly consistent, but the tradition varies from denomination to denomination and even from church to church.

Many traditional Stations of the Cross feature fourteen stations that are based on a mix of scripture and legend. Other traditions use nine stations—representing only those moments clearly articulated in scripture. I started with nine stations, but as I delved into the project, I discovered a series of fourteen stations, all based on scripture.

This was a gold mine for me. I was especially excited about the inclusion of the encounters leading up to the trial and condemnation by Pontius Pilate. It was also liberating to realize that I had options about stations to include. Since this was to be a metaphoric exploration, and not one held firmly in tradition, I could let my intuition guide me.

At one point, I chose eleven stations to paint. In retrospect, it never seemed completely right to have an odd number, but I was stymied. I now realize that, as is often the case in the creative process, a bit more gestation was taking place. I was experiencing the creative pause.

Another significant factor in the process was that the church where the stations would be displayed was going through some internal changes. The new interim priest was Friar Leo M. Joseph, a Franciscan friar. Up to this point, I had pretty much been working in a vacuum. The former priest was supportive but distant, the building and grounds committee was never really involved, and the benefactors wanted to give me complete freedom to create as I saw

VIII   IX   X   XI   XII   XIII   XIV

fit. This was fine to a point, but I was ready for some other input. It was serendipitous that a Franciscan friar was now involved in the project. The Franciscans have a close association with the Stations of the Cross. In fact, one tradition holds that it is necessary to have the stations blessed by a Franciscan before they are liturgically acceptable. This was territory that Friar Leo knew very well.

As always, God's timing was perfect, and Friar Leo's history and insight proved to be invaluable. "You can't just stop with eleven," he said. "It just isn't right to have an odd number." I knew he was right and that it was time to reenter the process. As I wrote in my journal during that time, "So, I guess that the stations aren't finished after all." I think the short break was important: it gave me the opportunity to take a fresh look at the series and helped me to gain a different perspective.

In a sense, this new view of the cross is at the heart of this station. We view Christ, as we view life, from the foot of the cross. This is the station of compassion, of the new family born of Christ. Familial ties are superseded by the new reality Christ pours out on the world. The focus begins to shift from the cross to Jesus' followers and those who love him. In other words, the focus shifts to us. This is the precursor to the new life that we will fully experience in the Resurrection, when everything changes. But for now, it is our perspective and our sense of family and community that begin to undergo a radical shift.

I was particularly moved by this station when I realized the larger implications—it was not just John and the women who formed a new family, it is all of us. We all yearn for family, true family, where we feel loved and accepted unconditionally. For a few of us, this is a reality within our biological family, but for many of us, it is not. And even if we are blessed with a loving family, we inevitably encounter disappointments and problems with one another. After all, families are made up of people, and people are, well, people. If we rely solely on our limited human abilities to love and to support one another, we will fall short. And if we depend on other people for unfailing love and support, we will sooner or later be disappointed. Jesus' life and passion create a different landscape for relationships, a landscape grounded in universal, selfless love.

We, with Mary and John, stand at the foot of the cross. If we keep our eyes fixed on Jesus, our perspective changes. I am reminded of the practice of Centering Prayer. In this practice, we enter the stillness inside, where there are no words or images, simply the presence of God—stillness that surrounds, comforts, and guides us. As we make this practice part of our daily life, we see that words— explanations, rationales, excuses—eventually fall away. Our life in Christ, at the foot of the cross, becomes the new paradigm, the new basis for our relationship to one another. The light of Christ illuminates and changes not only us but also the entire landscape of our lives.

PRAYER

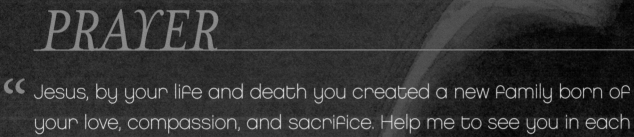

" Jesus, by your life and death you created a new family born of your love, compassion, and sacrifice. Help me to see you in each of my sisters and brothers. May we all know that we are one in you. **Amen.** "

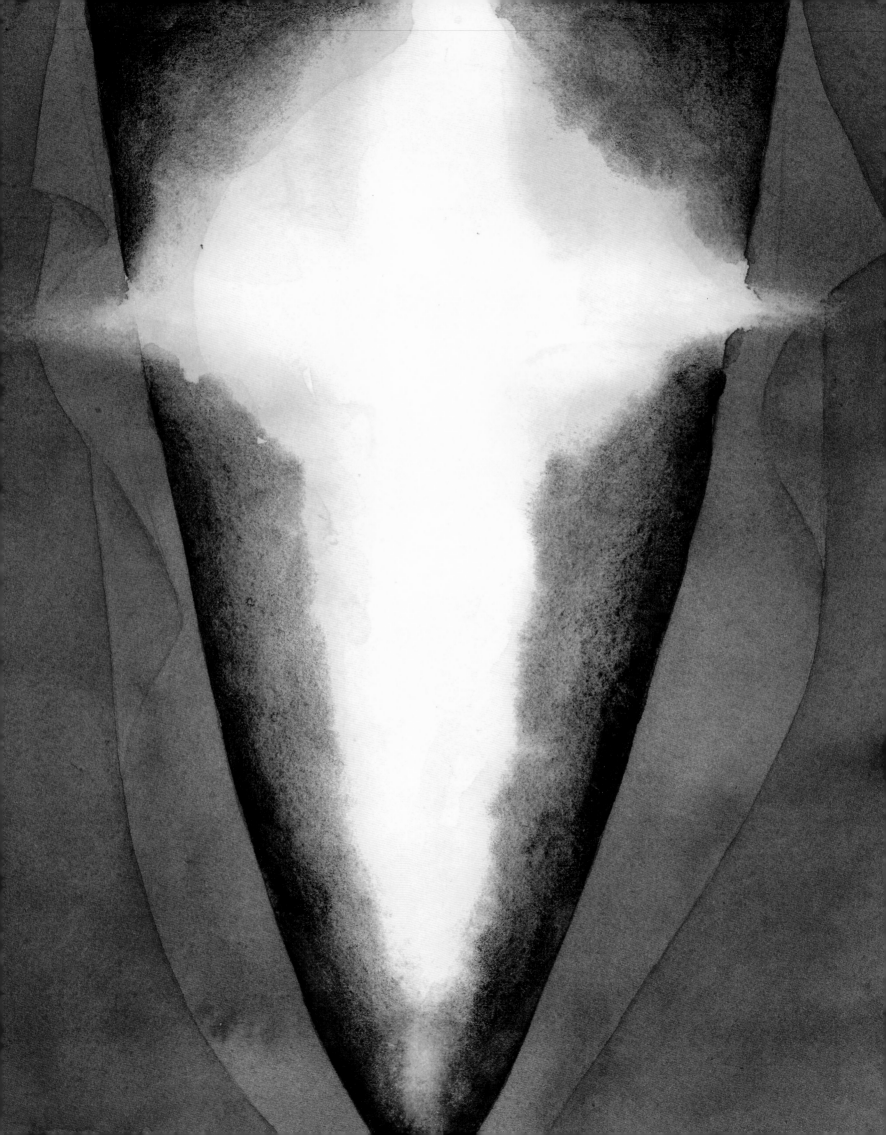

JESUS DIES XI
ON THE CROSS

From noon on, darkness came over the whole land until three in the afternoon. And about three o'clock Jesus cried with a loud voice, "Eli, Eli, lema sabachthani?" that is, "My God, my God, why have you forsaken me?" When some of the bystanders heard it, they said, "This man is calling for Elijah." At once one of them ran and got a sponge, filled it with sour wine, put it on a stick, and gave it to him to drink. But the others said, "Wait, let us see whether Elijah will come to save him." Then Jesus cried again with a loud voice and breathed his last. At that moment the curtain of the temple was torn in two, from top to bottom. The earth shook, and the rocks were split.

– Matthew 27:45-51

The veil between the sanctuary of the temple and the holy of holies is rent asunder from top to bottom. All that separated creation from the Creator is obliterated by the Almighty. The cherubim sheathe their swords as the gates of paradise are once and for all time flung wide. Let me never set anything between the Divine Presence and myself. May I strive to keep the awareness of my communion with God unobscured by any thing or person, especially my own ego, lest I fall prey to the deception of the deceiver as did our forebearers.

As Jesus' sacrificial death opened the way for me and for all of creation, may I rejoice in his unbounded love even in my darkest days, even now as I endure my own illness and impending death. Let this love make it possible for me to face my own passing from this life without fear and to embrace it with joyful anticipation. May I see in death not the end of life but the fulfillment of life. May Jesus' voluntary acceptance of his father's will help me to better prepare for a holy death and to be more fully aware of it as an entrance into the bosom of God the Father.

At the moment Jesus breathed forth his spirit, the eclipse of the sun caused a darkness to fall over the earth just as the "formless void and darkness covered the face of the deep" on the first day of creation (Genesis 1:2). When Jesus gave up his spirit, all creation ceased, and in the same moment the cosmos was recreated as the "earth shook, and the rocks were split" (Matthew 27:51). Nature's cosmic convulsions are the death throes of one era, and the birth pangs portend the age to come.

Let me order my affairs while I am still able so that after my death, my resources will enable the spread of the gospel just as Jesus preached the Good News of liberation to the righteous multitudes. "...one of the soldiers pierced his side with a spear, and at once blood and water came out." As the tide of blood and water that flowed from Jesus cleansed the face of the earth of its hopeless cycle of violence, so may the ocean of his relentless love absorb from me all traces of hatred and the defiance of will.

As Jesus' cross, thrust into the bosom of Mother Earth, unleashes the healing tide of love, so may it cleanse me and all humanity of its primal separation from our Divine Source.

Our sense of futility is banished and humankind's awareness of its true purpose is restored as the rending from top to bottom of the temple veil opens the way once more to our return home.

FRIAR LEO M. JOSEPH

I   II   III   IV   V   VI   VII

DEATH

Jesus dies. This is the moment when reality gets turned upside down. We ask ourselves, how can this happen? How can this man who lived a life of love and compassion die in this way?

We have already seen that he faced injustice and pain, but now this horrible death? Once again, the story shakes our preconceptions of the way things are supposed to be, and we are forced to take another look. If Jesus is indeed divine, then how could it come to this? Throughout the entire Way of the Cross, we have been faced with challenges to the status quo, just as his disciples had been. They had expected their messiah to be a warrior, someone who would change the system from without, using the same tactics of military might and political power that people had used throughout history, certainly throughout Jewish history. But from the beginning, Jesus was different.

Remember, it has only been a matter of days since Jesus rode triumphantly into Jerusalem on a donkey. That scenario sets the stage for the events that follow. After all, a savior, a king, doesn't ride on a donkey.

But then, a savior is not to be treated as a criminal either. Nothing about Jesus and his life, including his parables, made for easy understanding. His reality and message are at a deeper level and speak to the heart in the non-linear and sometimes paradoxical language of wisdom. Only by setting aside our need for rational explanations can we grasp the truth underlying the contradiction of Jesus' final moments and words, and ultimately, the truth and meaning of his life.

In Matthew and Mark's accounts, we hear Jesus cry out 'My God, my God, why have you forsaken me?' At first glance, this seems to be a cry of hopelessness and despair, and of course these emotions must have been a part of Jesus' experience. But, the words also are the first line of Psalm 22, a song of hope and confidence in ultimate victory. Jesus was an observant Jew, steeped in scripture and tradition. He and many others of that time would have been conscious of the layers of meaning to this cry. Once again we are thrown into the arena of multiple meanings, paradox, and mystery.

Yet, the fact remains that Jesus cries out in despair to God. We have already witnessed the betrayal and abandonment by his friends and disciples and by the Jewish community. But now God? If Jesus can feel abandoned by God, what does that say to the rest of us?

But within the gospel texts, we find hope. "At that moment the curtain of the temple was torn in two, from top to bottom. The earth shook, and the rocks were split." In the Jewish temple, the curtain or veil separated the holy, sacred part of the temple from the people. God was inaccessible and apart. But now, with Jesus' death, the division between the sacred and the secular, between the temporal and the eternal, was no more. The veil was torn in two from top to bottom, and the divine burst forth. Heaven and earth became one, and all of creation trembled.

I tremble when I think of it—that moment when Jesus shed his earthly body and became one with God. In doing so, Jesus tore down the barrier that separates us from God and from one another. His body died, but something else took its place—the promise of everlasting life. At that moment, life unfettered by physical or temporal constraints became a reality for each of us. Jesus transcended the limitations of the physical body and Jesus of Nazareth was free to become Jesus the Christ.

PRAYER

"Jesus, at your death, the curtain was torn, and heaven and earth became one. Fill my heart with your love and guide me that I may help to break down the walls that divide us. May your spirit flow through me as a healing force in this troubled world. **Amen.**"

XII

JESUS' BODY IS TAKEN DOWN FROM THE CROSS

Since it was the day of Preparation, the Jews did not want the bodies left on the cross during the sabbath, especially because that sabbath was a day of great solemnity. So they asked Pilate to have the legs of the crucified men broken and the bodies removed. Then the soldiers came and broke the legs of the first and of the other who had been crucified with him. But when they came to Jesus and saw that he was already dead, they did not break his legs. Instead, one of the soldiers pierced his side with a spear, and at once blood and water came out. After these things, Joseph of Arimathea, who was a disciple of Jesus, though a secret one because of his fear of the Jews, asked Pilate to let him take away the body of Jesus. Pilate gave him permission; so he came and removed his body.

– John 19:31-34,38

The half light belonging to neither day nor night hangs like a pall over Calvary's bleak hill. After the shaking of the earth, the jeering crowds and curious onlookers have fled for the safety of their homes, leaving you surrounded only with the loyal few. Joseph of Arimathea and the secret disciple, Nicodemus, remove the lifeless body of your dear Son from the cross and you gently enfold your maternal arms around the fruit of your womb. The prophetic words of aged Simeon uttered in the holy temple echo in your mind:

"This child is destined for the falling and the rising of many in Israel, and to be a sign that will be opposed so that the inner thoughts of many will be revealed—and a sword will pierce your own soul too." How indeed a sword now pierces your heart as your bitter tears mingle with his congealing blood.

Before breathing forth his spirit, your son commended his beloved disciple to you saying, "Woman, here is your son." May I who strive to be his disciple experience your maternal love and solicitude in all my trials. He also gave you into the disciple's care saying, "Here is your mother." Help me to comfort you in your sorrow by embracing the grief of all mothers who weep and mourn for the loss of their offspring.

May I behold you in the mother kneeling on a trash-strewn ghetto street, weeping over the corpse of her child shot in a senseless gang shooting; the mother kneeling beside a hospital bed, cradling the body of her young son who has just died of AIDS; the mother throwing herself over the casket delivered from the belly of a military transport plane.

May this image of the *Pieta* once more melt the coldness of all our hearts, which have become hardened to the pain and anguish of mothers worldwide who bore us for joy and fullness of life.

Give me voice to cry out with the words of the prophet Jeremiah: "A voice was heard in Ramah, wailing and loud lamentation, Rachel weeping for her children; she refused to be consoled, because they are no more" (Matthew 2:18).

FRIAR LEO M. JOSEPH

LOVE

This is the one station where I strayed from using a strictly scriptural approach to the series. Mary, the mother of Jesus, is not mentioned in the scriptural account of Jesus' body being removed from the cross, and it is unlikely that she was there to cradle him in her arms. Still, in this case it seemed appropriate to turn to legend.

I was encouraged to this by Friar Leo, the Franciscan friar who was a guide and mentor in this process. It was important from a pastoral point of view to include an image that spoke directly to personal loss and grief. I wanted to include an image that brought the poignancy and pain of the loss into sharp focus. Parents who lose a child say that it is the worst experience imaginable, that the grief never goes away. Add to this the circumstances of her son's death, and Mary's grief and sadness are beyond description.

Like most artists, I have certain images that keep showing up in my work. They change and evolve but eventually spiral back around and appear without my consciously planning it.

Existentialist Albert Camus once said, "A man's work is nothing but this slow trek to rediscover, through the detours of art, those two or three great and simple images in whose presence his heart first opened."

During those transcendent—and rare—moments when we truly become conscious of things beyond ourselves, our hearts open. For these sometimes fleeting moments, we are no longer alone and apart but rather one with all of creation.

Light is a recurring image in my work, perhaps inspired by the sunrises over the mountains near where I was born. I remember mornings as a small child standing on our front porch, watching the sun slowly appear over the Sonoma Mountains, the soft yellow light bathing the dusky, lavender hills with a warm glow. It marked the beginning of a new day, and, in retrospect, the beginning of my young life as well. Without consciously intending it, a glow eventually turns up in most of my paintings. Whether the subject is flowers, landscapes, or people, I can't seem to help myself. I paint along, and then there it is, a bit of a glow and then a burst of light. I've learned to accept it. In the Way of the Cross series, the light is Christ, the eternal glow that illuminates and blesses.

Many years ago, I was in a graduate program in psychology while concurrently completing a master's degree in art. In retrospect, it was a harried and crazy period of my life, but in the midst of it, I was excited and inspired. I began to make real connections between spirit and psyche, art and process, and spirituality and creativity.

In the psychology program, I encountered a bias against Christianity that caught me completely off guard. The Jungian tradition of psychology uses dream work and metaphor, and from a spiritual perspective, interfaced nicely with my Christian faith. This approach to inner work often references other cultures and religions so our studies covered a variety of spiritual paths. It was a rich time, and I learned much about the common ground between different religions and spiritual approaches. Yet I also experienced firsthand the tendency of some segments of contemporary culture to denigrate Christianity. It was unsettling to say the least. Pagan approaches and ideology were celebrated, while Christianity was nearly always criticized, even ridiculed. Perhaps my skin was a little thin, but after a few months it got tedious. I felt increasingly isolated and defensive.

One afternoon, I had an especially unpleasant experience with a professor.

I felt as if the ground had closed up over me, and I was being held in the arms of the earth where it was dark and comforting. This image came from deep within my psyche, and I later created a series of paintings based on it. As the image grew and evolved, it became that of a nun, diffusely painted, gazing inward and seeing the cosmos. Going into and exploring the depths renewed my realization of a greater reality. I was no longer the center of the universe. As my anger and frustration gave way to acceptance and compassion, the feeling of aloneness became a feeling of oneness.

As I began to paint this station, I realized the image from my graduate school days held the seeds of the Pieta. As Mary, engulfed in grief, held her dead child, she also held eternity in her arms, just as she had held eternity in her womb before he was born. At the Annunciation, she expressed her surrender to the Archangel Gabriel—"Here am I, the servant of the Lord; let it be with me according to your word" (Luke 1:38). She surrendered to the will of God and in doing so, accepted her destiny. She accepted this child as she accepted his death—as a bearer of the light and a servant of God.

In the iconic tradition, Mary is referred to as the *Theotokos*, the God bearer. We are all called to be God bearers as we live our lives in and through him. Mary's obedience and devotion are the ultimate example of how surrender to God's will brings Christ's love into the world.

Mary accepted her role in God's plan, just as we are called to accept ours. As we see in the Way of the Cross, this is never an easy task. Yet through surrender and acceptance, we are able to be open to the depths of Christ's love, to embrace and carry it, and through our lives, do our part to help the light shine forth into the world.

PRAYER

"Divine Comforter, be with me in times of grief and despair. Comfort those who mourn. Hold me in your loving arms. **Amen.**"

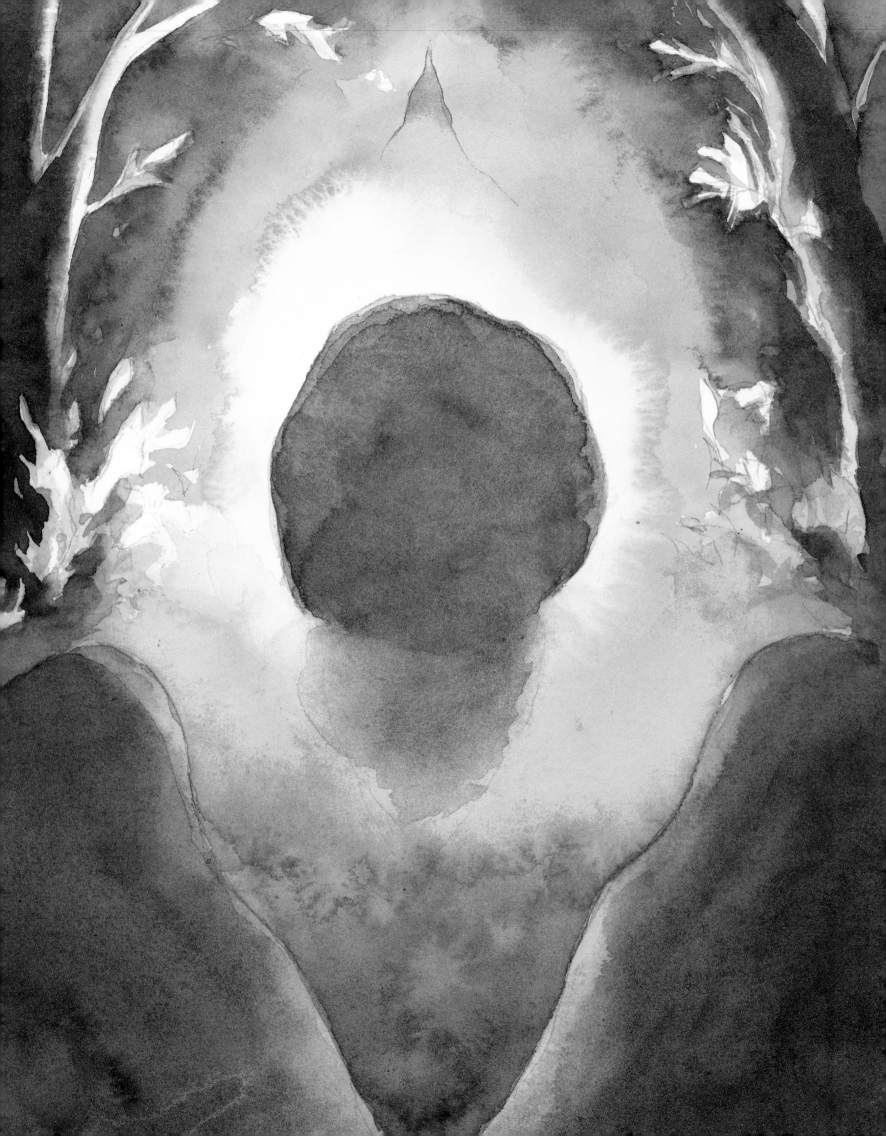

JESUS' BODY XIII IS ENTOMBED

So Joseph took the body and wrapped it in a clean linen
cloth and laid it in his own new tomb, which he had hewn
in the rock. He then rolled a great stone to the door
of the tomb and went away. Mary Magdalene and the
other Mary were there, sitting opposite the tomb.

— Matthew 27:59-61

They took the body of Jesus and wrapped it with the
spices in linen cloths, according to the burial custom of
the Jews. Now there was a garden in the place where
he was crucified, and in the garden there was a new
tomb in which no one had ever been laid. And so,
because it was the Jewish day of Preparation, and
the tomb was nearby, they laid Jesus there.

— John 19:40-42

The passion has dimmed but not gone out. Its focus will rest in the tomb, outwardly less ardent but not extinguished. The grief outside the tomb is sacrament of the fire that still burns in the heart of God. The rock tomb will be womb—overturned—the life and heat within grown cool. The tendrils of life are still present, though they, too, have been turned and reversed, to infuse life again into what seems dead to the world. The tunnel of life is stopped for a season; the valve of the heart momentarily closed, awaiting the beat of new life.

And whom do we find here, at this valve-stop? Joseph, who offers to shield a life not of his own creation—he yields his place to one in greater need of it. The body of the most vulnerable is once again swaddled close, like the enfolding arms of God or the husk of a seed that must bide its time in the earth until it springeth green once more. And like Mary and Elizabeth once before, the Marys wait again for new life to emerge—either in their own hearts or, hoping against hope, from this closed-mouth tomb.

The world continues expectant at tombs. The faithful fosterers and harborers of life, men and women who follow the impassioned one, continue to seek more abundant life, even at the valve-stops of this world. They see the greenness already present, hidden though it may be from more casual glances. They have given their hearts to the beat of the one who plants life everywhere and insists that it has created all for abundance.

Will we sit at the tombs with those who wait, expectant? Will we offer up our place for the vulnerable among us? After all is said and done, solidarity and passion are the only gifts we have to offer at this cave.

Presiding Bishop
Katharine Jefferts Schori

WAITING

John's Gospel is the only account that mentions the tomb in a garden. As is often the case with John, his descriptions are poetic and full of metaphor.

The other gospels give us the who, what, when, and where, but John often gives us a way to imagine into the stories of Christ, to grasp with our hearts and not simply our minds. And so, we come full circle back to a garden, a place generally associated with growth and bounty—a place of new life and new beginnings. In the Garden of Gethsemane, Jesus prayed for help and support, and the angel appeared to him and gave him strength. In this garden however, we are told of a different kind of presence—of Mary Magdalene and the other Mary. The two women don't flee as the disciples had; they are simply there, waiting. This station is one of stillness and waiting. We have had the condemnation, the long walk to Calvary, the trauma of the crucifixion, and now the body is in the tomb, and time stands still. We, along with the women, wait.

Throughout the stations, we often see women in the role of witness to the life and passion of Christ. When Jesus meets the women of Jerusalem on the way to Golgotha, or Mary cradles his body in her arms, or now, when the two Marys sit at the tomb in silence, the women are present. They do not flee or turn away. They are simply there. But it would be a mistake to limit this to merely a statement on gender. It is about the archetypically feminine way of being in the world. Some of the qualities of the feminine are receptivity, being as opposed to doing, and intuition— qualities these women represent with their steadfast presence. Jesus was revolutionary in his acceptance of women. But another critical teaching of his life was celebrating this way of interacting with other people, of surrender, acceptance, and tolerance. This messiah turned the world upside down by doing the

unexpected. In a patriarchal society, he not only accepted and honored women. He also embraced and taught another way of being.

Try to imagine the tomb without the presence of the women. I can't. Their presence completes the experience, and they are an integral part of the transformation. So often in times of distress or hurt, we want to do something for someone, to fix the problem.

We offer advice or help or try to think of something we can do, when in reality the most helpful thing that we can do is to simply be there, just as these women were at the cross and now at the tomb. Their quiet presence speaks volumes about their devotion and their faith. Through them, we are drawn into the experience. They, and we, are the witnesses to the miracle that is now in gestation.

In this garden, the body of Jesus lies buried—a seed holding the promise of new life. These two women wait in silence as all of creation prepares for the burst of glory that is to come.

But for now, on this Holy Saturday, the world waits.

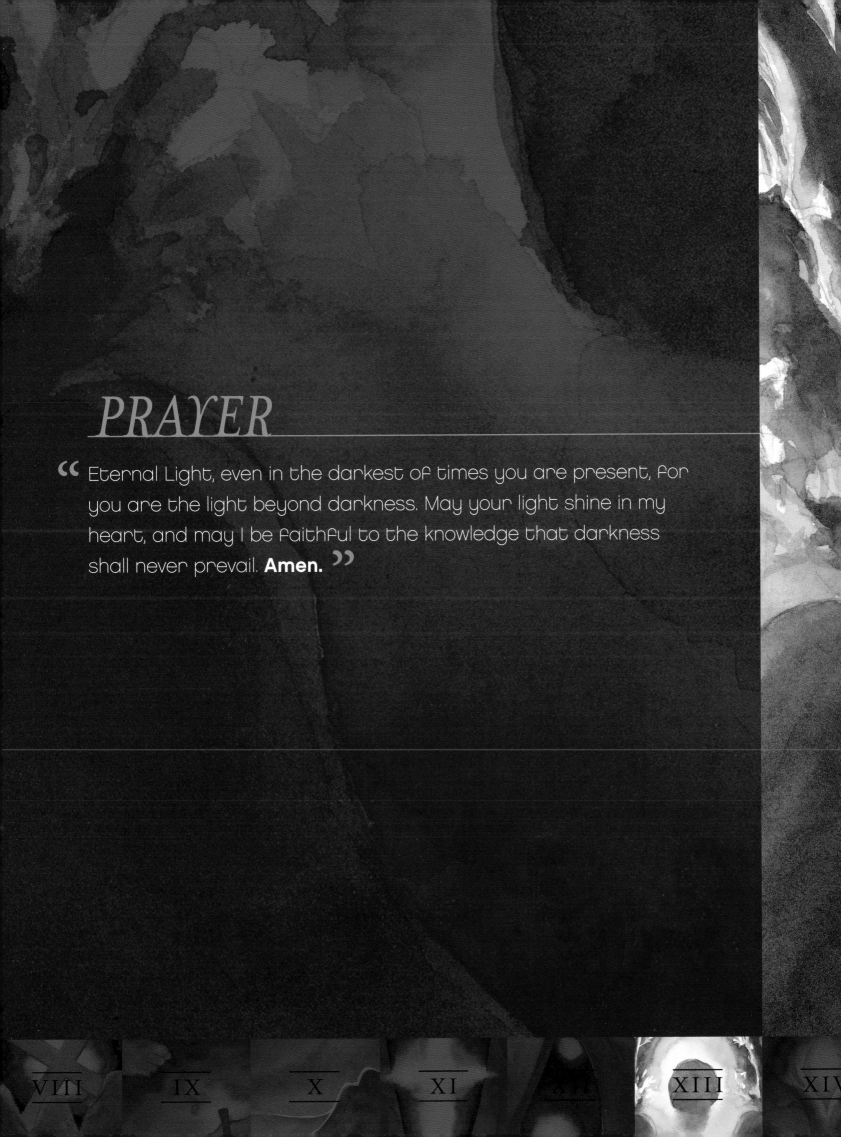

PRAYER

"Eternal Light, even in the darkest of times you are present, for you are the light beyond darkness. May your light shine in my heart, and may I be faithful to the knowledge that darkness shall never prevail. **Amen.**"

THE LORD IS RISEN XIV

After the sabbath, as the first day of the week was dawning, Mary Magdalene and the other Mary went to see the tomb. And suddenly there was a great earthquake; for an angel of the Lord, descending from heaven, came and rolled back the stone and sat on it. His appearance was like lightning, and his clothing white as snow. For fear of him the guards shook and became like dead men. But the angel said to the women, "Do not be afraid; I know that you are looking for Jesus who was crucified. He is not here; for he has been raised, as he said. Come, see the place where he lay. Then go quickly and tell his disciples, 'He has been raised from the dead, and indeed he is going ahead of you to Galilee; there you will see him.' This is my message for you." So they left the tomb quickly with fear and great joy, and ran to tell his disciples. Suddenly, Jesus met them and said, "Greetings!" And they came to him, took hold of his feet, and worshiped him. Then Jesus said to them, "Do not be afraid; go and tell my brothers to go to Galilee; there they will see me."

– Matthew 28:1-10

The gospel stories of the Passion, Death, and Resurrection of Jesus begin and end in a garden that roots him firmly to the earth. The imagery of the paintings by Kathrin beautifully ties together the first and last of the Stations of the Cross. In the first station, we see Jesus' agony in the garden where he sought comfort in the trees that overarched and protected him as he struggled with the difficult decision he was called to make. In the final station, the Risen Christ's journey culminates in another garden, where the Tree of the Cross is transfigured into a Tree of Life.

The hymn, "Sing, my tongue, the glorious battle", recounts, "One and only noble tree! None in foliage, none in blossom, none in fruit thy peer may be." The divine light and energy of love radiates throughout the universe, uniting and interconnecting all of creation. In the first image, the trees seem to enclose the light, but in the final image, that light is bursting forth freely.

That awesome burst of love and energy infused the lives of all of the friends and disciples whom Jesus had touched. They were transfigured, changed forever. They did not know how or why, but they knew their beloved friend was alive with them and within them, filling them with love and surrounding them, bringing a joy and purpose they had never known was possible. They would echo with Mary, "The Lord is Risen!" That cry has echoed on down through the centuries as Christians everywhere celebrate the mystery of Resurrection.

That transformation spreads throughout all of creation in undulating waves of energy of divine light and love. It begins, perhaps, at the very moment when Christ's light and love encompasses Mary of Magdala in the garden before the tomb and radiates out from her in a great flaring forth. The divine energy of love flows through her to the other disciples in ever-widening circles of incredibly transforming energy—love's ultimate victory over death. But this journey is not without fear, resistance, and great cost on the part of those who carry the message. This struggle and sacrifice may be represented in the splotches of red on the trunk of the tree.

The tree of life is a powerful and universal symbol of incarnation, with its roots reaching deep into the earth, bringing energy and strength to the whole tree. The branches reach out in intricate patterns in all directions, seeking light and nourishment, reminding us that the Resurrection is a part of the whole flowering of new life that runs deep into the one source—the Divine Mystery of Love. Alleluia!

SISTER TERESA MARIE MARTIN

RESURRECTION

Mary Magdalene and the other Mary go to the tomb to care for Jesus' body. One can only imagine their grief over what has happened to their friend and teacher. Not only have they lost their beloved Jesus, but they also have lost hope in what might have been, in the promises he embodied.

Then they encounter something quite unexpected—an angel at the tomb. In the Gospel of Matthew, the appearance of the angel is quite dramatic, heralded by yet another earthquake. When Jesus died on the cross, the earth shook and the skies darkened, and this moment summons the same earth-shaking response. This is the moment when Jesus' followers learn the story isn't over, that in fact, it might just be beginning.

The angel's appearance is quite impressive—an earthquake announces his arrival, he looks like lightning, and his clothing is white as snow. He may be a heavenly messenger, but this is scary stuff. Anyone who has experienced an earthquake knows they are frightening. I've lived most of my life on the San Andreas Fault in California and have felt many tremors over the years. I still find each one terrifying. When the quake hits and the earth shakes and the buildings sway, I feel deep inside a direct encounter with God, tectonic plates notwithstanding. It's no wonder we call such events "Acts of God." Add to that the angel's appearance, which is like lightning, and this messenger has our attention. In fact, it's so scary that the guards collapse in fear.

An angel, a messenger from God, makes two appearances in the Way of the Cross. In the first station, an angel appears before Jesus in the Garden of Gesthemane and gives him strength. And now, the angel appears a second time, again to give strength, telling the women to not be afraid, that Jesus "has been raised, as he said."

Even more than strength the angel gives the women courage. He admonishes them to fear not, which reminds us of the words of Gabriel to Mary at the Annunciation. "Do not be afraid Mary, for you have found favor with God" (Luke 1:30). An angel announces the conception of Jesus into the earthly life, and an angel appears now again, as Jesus enters eternal life.

Angels, God's messengers, are present not to work miracles or to change events but to comfort and encourage. In times of trouble, we often feel as if we are on our own. If we can muster our faith, we trust in God and God's Word, but we are alone nevertheless. And it can be frightening. Perhaps angels are there all along, but walking the Way of the Cross means relying on the promise of God's presence, proceeding in faith, even during those times when we are gripped by fear, and angels are nowhere to be seen. Mary bore and raised Jesus, trusting in the promise of God as delivered by Gabriel; Jesus walked the Way of the Cross to his death, trusting in God; and Mary Magdalene and the other women didn't flee or give up on Jesus. They went to the tomb. They needed to show up in order to hear the Good News. It seems that angels appear when we are ready to hear their message. But, before we can hear the message, we need to show up, and this is where faith comes in.

Yet there's much more to faith than showing up. Even after hearing the message that Jesus was risen, they left with fear and great joy. What are we to make of this fear? Do we feel fear at the resurrection and the reality of the risen Christ? Perhaps we should. Truth can be scary stuff. And with the Resurrection of Jesus, the world turned upside down. Life and death would never be viewed in quite the same way. Annie Dillard says it well in *Teaching a Stone to Talk*, "It is madness to wear ladies' straw hats and velvet hats to church; we should all be wearing crash helmets. Ushers should issue life preservers and signal flares; they should lash us to our pews."

Indeed. No wonder an angel shows up to help. The angel urges us past our all-too-human response of fear to the amazing new reality of the Resurrection. Death as we know it has been vanquished, and our relationship with the Divine, with eternity, will never be the same. There is nothing to fear, because we now know that Christ, the spirit of the risen Lord, the author of creation, is always with us. The image of the tree with the burst of light shows the glory of the Divine that infuses all of creation. We are free to experience the eternal held in each moment and to witness God's presence all around us.

The Resurrection tells us that things are not always as they seem, or as we have believed. Dying to self, we find new life. We die; we are reborn. Over and over again. But each time, perhaps ever so slightly, something changes. New life can come in small increments or in a burst of glory. But each step of the Way, God is with us.

PRAYER

" Risen Lord, be with me always as I walk each step of The Way. Open my eyes to your divine glory in all of creation and fill my heart with the joy of your eternal presence. **Amen.** "

ABOUT THE ARTIST

Kathrin Burleson is an artist and writer. She was born in Petaluma, California, and has lived most of her life in Northern California. She holds a bachelor of arts degree in French from the University of California, Berkeley, as well as advanced degrees in art and psychology. She studied art and art history at the Louvre in Paris while pursuing her studies in French literature at the Sorbonne.

The common thread in her background and current work is communication—the connections between realms and the bridges between realities. Themes of her paintings range from conceptual and contemplative works to visionary interpretations of the natural world. Whether painting people, animals, or liturgical themes, her work explores the interconnectedness of all of creation. The recipient of numerous awards, she has exhibited her work in museums, galleries, and churches throughout the United States.

Kathrin was baptized Greek Orthodox, raised in a Presbyterian church, and became an Episcopalian as a young adult. She is grateful for this rich variety of religious experience and finds meaning and beauty in each of these traditions. She is a founding member of Saints Martha and Mary Episcopal Mission, Trinidad, and is an associate of the Community of the Transfiguration, a religious community for women in The Episcopal Church.

Kathrin and her husband Michael live in Trinidad, California, where they share their home with a lively menagerie, which includes a talkative African grey parrot, an elderly cat, and two Pembroke Welsh corgis. When not painting or writing, she can usually be found training or running agility with her dogs.

View more of her work at www.KathrinBurleson.com.

ABOUT THE CONTRIBUTORS

THE RT. REV. BARRY LEIGH BEISNER

The Rt. Rev. Barry Leigh Beisner was elected the seventh bishop of the Diocese of Northern California in 2006. He was born in Ohio and raised in Southern California. He graduated from the University of California, Berkeley with a bachelor's degree in history and was elected to Phi Beta Kappa. He received a master of divinity degree in 1978 from The Church Divinity School of the Pacific; The General Theological Seminary awarded him a master of sacred theology degree in 1994 and a doctor of divinity degree in 2007.

Ordained a priest in 1975, he has served congregations in California and Ohio. In his ministry, he helped plant a new congregation and was instrumental in founding a program to feed and house the poor. He also served as an army reserve chaplain. He was named canon to the ordinary in the Diocese of Northern California in 2002.

He is a Benedictine oblate and an associate of the Community of the Transfiguration. He has been married to the Rev. L. Ann Hallisey since 1998, and together they have six grown children.

THE REV. ALBERTO R. CUTIÉ

The Rev. Alberto R. Cutié (also known as "Padre Alberto") has had the special privilege of entering millions of homes throughout the world through a variety of television and radio programs, as well as his books and advice columns. He became the first priest to conduct a daily "Talk Show" broadcast to a national and international audience. Originally ordained a Roman Catholic priest in 1995, Father Cutié joined The Episcopal Church in 2009 and now serves in the Diocese of Southeast Florida.

He is the author of *Real Life, Real Love (Ama de Verdad, Vive de Verdad)*, a self-help book that became a bestseller in Spanish. His latest book, *Dilemma*, is a candid and controversial memoir about faith and love. He currently serves The Church of the Resurrection in Biscayne Park, Florida, where he lives with his wife, Ruhama, and their three children. Father Cutié's new radio segment is entitled "Animo Para el Camino" (Courage for the Journey) and offers an inspirational message for daily living. His website is www.padrealberto.com.

THE REV. CANON SCOTT GUNN

The Rev. Canon Scott Gunn is executive director of Forward Movement, where he joins in the venerable organization's ministry of creating and sharing resources for discipleship and evangelism. Prior to this ministry, he served as a parish priest in the Diocese of Rhode Island. Before ordination, he worked in information technology for a variety of corporations and nonprofit organizations, including the MIT Media Lab, IBM, *The Atlantic Monthly*, and Education Development Center.

In churchwide ministry, Father Gunn serves as a deputy to General Convention and has served on several committees. He travels widely throughout the church as a speaker, preacher, and teacher. He lives in Cincinnati with his spouse, the Rev. Canon Sherilyn Pearce, who serves as the canon pastor at Christ Church Cathedral. He blogs at www.sevenwholedays.org and tweets are at @scottagunn.

THE MOST REV. KATHARINE JEFFERTS SCHORI

The Most Rev. Katharine Jefferts Schori was elected as the twenty-sixth presiding bishop of The Episcopal Church in June 2006. She serves as chief pastor and primate to The Episcopal Church's members in sixteen countries and 110 dioceses. She joins with other bishops of the worldwide Anglican Communion, seeking a common cause for global good and reconciliation.

Over the course of her nine-year term, the presiding bishop has been vocal about The Episcopal Church's mission priorities, including the United Nations' Millennium Development Goals, issues of domestic poverty, climate change and care for the earth, as well as the ongoing need to contextualize the gospel.

Her career as an oceanographer preceded her studies for the priesthood, to which she was ordained in 1994. She holds a master's and doctorate degrees in oceanography from Oregon State University, a master of divinity degree from Church Divinity School of the Pacific, and several honorary doctoral degrees. She remains an active, instrument-rated pilot.

She grew up in the Seattle area and has spent most of her life in the West. She and her husband, Richard Miles Schori, a retired mathematician (topologist), were married in 1979. They have one daughter, who is a captain (pilot) in the U.S. Air Force, and a grandson.

Friar Leo M. Joseph, OSF

Friar Leo M. Joseph, OSF, (Leo Joseph Brown) is the priest-in-charge of St. John's Episcopal Church in Lakeport, California. Born in Brooklyn, New York, he entered a Mariavite Old Catholic Franciscan religious community in New York City and received the Franciscan habit in 1972.

Friar Leo was ordained a priest in Montreal. While continuing his work as an ecclesiastical designer for C.M. Almy, he served as a priest at The Church of the Beloved Disciple in New York City and was active in the emerging gay and lesbian rights movement.

In 1979 he relocated to San Francisco, California. As the AIDS epidemic emerged in the early 1980s, he began ministering to the dying and their families in San Francisco. In 1985, Friar Leo arranged the purchase of the property in Kelseyville, California, that would become Little Portion Hermitage. In 1995, he was received into The Episcopal Church as a life-professed religious, and two years later, as a priest. He served several congregations in the Bay Area. In 2009, he returned to the Hermitage and was named priest-in-charge of St. John's in Lakeport, California. A year later, he was diagnosed with incurable cancer and given three months to live. He continues to minister and serve God at St. John's.

Sister Teresa Marie Martin, CT

Sister Teresa Marie Martin, CT, is superior of the Community of the Transfiguration, a religious community for women in The Episcopal Church with headquarters in Cincinnati, Ohio. She is a native of Berkeley, California, and a graduate of the University of California, Berkeley, with a major in geography. She also holds master's degrees in education and theology from Xavier University in Cincinnati.

Sister Teresa served as a teacher and principal of Bethany, the Community's school in Cincinnati, for a number of years before returning to California in 1980 where she was a retreat and workshop leader as part of the Community's ministry on the West Coast.

In 2008 she was elected superior of the Community and returned to Cincinnati when she presently resides. Creation-centered spirituality and the new universe story are passions for her, integrating her love of spirituality, science, art, and nature.

ACKNOWLEDGEMENTS

This book has evolved over several years and has been quite a journey. As with many journeys, the path twisted and turned in ways I never imagined. Fortunately, I was blessed to have the right companions along the way. There were those who sent me off with good wishes, friends who accompanied me part of the way, fellow travelers that I met along the path, and some who I have only met recently through their writing. Together we formed a community that created and contributed to this book—a band of pilgrims exploring the landscape of our faith.

Friar Leo M. Joseph has been a guide and mentor throughout most of this journey. It's hard to think of a bearded friar clad in a worn traditional Franciscan habit as an angel, but he really seemed like one when he offered just the right insight, advice, or encouragement to keep me going. A brilliant and wise man, he is a gifted teacher and treasured friend. In 2010, he was diagnosed with incurable cancer and given months to live. Incredibly, without any medical treatment, he continues to serve his parish, write, and minister. With his usual wit, he says he is way past his expiration date and notes that his hospice worker says that he is her only client who has officiated at four funerals while under her care. It is especially poignant and meaningful that he was able to contribute to this book. "Don't worry, Kathrin. I'll stick around till I get it written." Throughout his ministry, his life has been an example of how to live with grace and faith, and now his dying is no different. His friendship is a blessing and his life of faith an inspiration.

Sister Teresa Marie Martin has been a friend and fellow traveler for many years. When she was still serving in the nearby Branch House of the Community of the Transfiguration, of which I am an associate, we both belonged to the *Gyrovagues*, a small group of seekers who would gather monthly for mutual support and encouragement. The name of the group, Gyrovagues, comes from Saint Benedict. He described certain monks as gyrovagues: "Always on the move, they never settle down, and are slaves to their own wills and gross appetites." And while we perhaps weren't that bad, we did find plenty to talk about and work on. As shown in her writing in these pages, Sister Teresa has the gift of clarity and she was often the one to offer a helpful insight into whatever challenge we might be facing. She has a wonderful, playful way with words.

Bishop Barry Beisner was a recently ordained priest when he officiated at my reception as an associate of the Community of the Transfiguration over twenty years ago. It has been a joy to watch his ministry unfold, and we in the Diocese of Northern California know how blessed we are to have a bishop of such faith and compassion. He continues to amaze and bless us with his many gifts, not the least of which is his ability to bring our faith into the here and now. His leadership helps to prepare and strengthen us to meet the challenges of being a Christian in these difficult times. As these pages show, his words are poetic and powerful.

Over ten years ago, as the Bishop of Nevada, Presiding Bishop Katharine Jefferts Schori was the keynote speaker at our Diocese of Northern California Convention. At that time, few of us knew her, but as soon as she began to speak, it was clear that we were listening to an extraordinary woman, and her tenure as Presiding Bishop has borne that out. Her ability to lead The Episcopal Church during these challenging times, all the while writing books and maintaining a personal pastoral presence, is remarkable.

In a very direct way, Father Scott Gunn has been involved with this book from nearly the beginning. Soon after Forward Movement approached me with the idea of this book, he took over the reins of the publishing company. He not only thinks outside the box in terms of concept, he also writes beautifully. This book would not have happened without him.

Father Alberto Cutié was known to me only through his books when we invited him to contribute to *The Soul's Journey.* We've had one telephone conversation, when at my editor's urging, I tracked him down and called to nag him about meeting the deadline for his meditations. Even then, when cornered by yet another responsibility and commitment, this busy pastor, writer, family man, and doctoral candidate was kind and obliging. And not surprisingly, his insights are wonderful (and submitted on time!).

Our companion and guide during the last part of the journey has been our editor, Richelle Thompson. She has been a patient and loving shepherd (emphasis on herd-ing) of this band of pilgrims as we wrote and submitted our meditations and reflections. She has the gifts of words, encouragement, and vision.

Finally, I can't imagine a better partner along the way than my husband Michael. His support and love sustain me. He listens patiently as I explore ideas and vent frustrations, has a gift for composition—both visual and verbal—and his suggestions are always spot on. My love and gratitude for him are boundless.

The original paintings of *The Way of the Cross* are in the Chapel of Our Merciful Savior, at Christ Episcopal Church, in Eureka, California. They are watercolor on paper, and 13 1/2 x 16 inches. Visitors and pilgrims are welcome.